Young Children in a Digi...

Young children are born into a digital world and it is not unusual to see preschool children intuitively swiping screens and confidently pressing buttons. There is much debate about the impact of the increased access to technology on young children's health and wellbeing with claims that it damages their social skills and emotional development. This timely new textbook examines how developments in technology, particularly mobile and touchscreen technology, have impacted on children's lives and how when used appropriately it can support all aspects of their development.

Clearly linking theory and research to everyday practice, the book offers guidance on:

- The role of technology in the early years curriculum
- Developing young children's understanding of safe and responsible use of technology
- The role of the adult within digital play activities
- Using technology to enhance and develop young children's creativity
- Technology and language acquisition

Featuring a wide range of case studies and examples to show how the ideas described can be put into practice, this is essential reading for all early years students and practitioners that want to know how they can harness technology in a meaningful way to support young children's learning and development.

Lorraine Kaye teaches students on undergraduate and postgraduate primary and early years teacher training programmes and is currently the subject leader for computing in primary and early years education at Middlesex University, UK.

Young Children in a Digital Age

Supporting learning and development with technology in early years

Edited by Lorraine Kaye

Routledge
Taylor & Francis Group

LONDON AND NEW YORK

First published 2017
by Routledge
2 Park Square, Milton Park, Abingdon, Oxon OX14 4RN

and by Routledge
711 Third Avenue, New York, NY 10017

Routledge is an imprint of the Taylor & Francis Group, an informa business

British Library Cataloguing in Publication Data
A catalogue record for this book is available from the British Library

Library of Congress Cataloging in Publication Data
Names: Kaye, Lorraine, author.
Title: Young children in a digital age : teaching and learning with technology in the early years / Lorraine Kaye.
Description: Abingdon, Oxon ; New York, NY : Routledge, [2016] | Includes index.
Identifiers: LCCN 2015047938| ISBN 9781138804791 (hardback) | ISBN 9781138804807 (pbk.) | ISBN 9781315752709 (ebook)
Subjects: LCSH: Educational technology--Great Britain. | Computer-assisted instruction--Great Britain. | Education, Elementary--Great Britain.
Classification: LCC LB1028.3 .K38 2016 | DDC 371.330941--dc23
LC record available at http://lccn.loc.gov/2015047938

ISBN: 978-1-138-80479-1 (hbk)
ISBN: 978-1-138-80480-7 (pbk)
ISBN: 978-1-315-75270-9 (ebk)

Typeset in Bembo and Helvetica Neue LT Pro
by Saxon Graphics Ltd, Derby

Contents

Acknowledgements

There are so many people I would like to thank for the writing and completion of this book. This includes the many nurseries and early years settings that made me feel so welcome on my visits and whose practice made a valuable contribution to the contents of the book. Particular thanks to Jodi McCallum and her staff at Hampden Way Nursery for allowing us to use her setting for the photographs and to Samuel Harding, the professional photographer, for the wonderful results. Thanks are also due to friends and colleagues who seemed very eager to provide other appropriate pictures of their grandchildren for inclusion in the book.

A special thank you to Margrethe who stepped in at short notice. Her chapter is a comprehensive discussion on the role of early years practitioners in relation to technology and provides a European perspective. The book would not have been possible without the support and dedication of many of the early years team at Middlesex University who have given their time and enthusiasm. Their chapters reflect their expertise and considerable knowledge in their fields.

Finally, my friends and family who I know I neglected during the process, particularly my husband, Michael, whose support is endless and my two wonderful children, Lynette and Neil. And, of course, my wonderful grandson Thomas (aged five) who was the perfect person to test out apps and discuss the pros and cons of tablet technology for me!

Contributors

Shirley Allen is programme leader for the Learning and Teaching programmes and Knowledge Transfer lead for Education at Middlesex University. She was a primary teacher for several years before moving to the University of Hertfordshire in 2005 to work on initial teacher training programmes. She moved to Middlesex University in 2007 to work as Senior Lecturer in Early Childhood Studies and programme leader for the Early Years Professional Status programme. Shirley has also worked on initial teacher training routes at Middlesex and written on the subject of early years pedagogy and practice.

Beverley Barnaby is a Senior Lecturer in Early Childhood Studies at Middlesex University. She has an MA in Education and a BEd (Hons). Throughout her professional life she has worked in pre-schools, primary schools, secondary schools and further education colleges, eventually specialising in early years education. This has involved working with children, parents, governors and fellow professionals from multidisciplinary agencies. She now leads modules on Early Childhood Development and Leadership in the Early Years. Her research interests are in critical thinking and assessment.

Victoria Burghardt is Programme Leader for the BA Early Childhood Studies Course at Middlesex University, and also a Senior Lecturer. She has a BSc (Hons) in Psychology and an MBA in Educational Management. Before becoming a university lecturer, she qualified as a primary teacher and also managed childcare courses within further education. She has recently qualified as a Forest School instructor. Her research interests are in nurturing critical and creative thinking through effective pedagogies.

Louise Dryden has worked for many years in schools, FE colleges and in the university sector. Her specialist area is in early years, with a focus on language development. Louise has taught, and trained practitioners extensively, and published on the subject. She has co-edited two textbooks on early years practice and written a number of articles and chapters on the development of language in young children.

Currently she is lecturing part-time at Middlesex University and supports UCL Institute of Education candidates on a School Direct programme.

Beth Gallagher has extensive experience of early years education and multi-agency partnerships, having been employed by voluntary and statutory sectors at home and overseas. She has been teaching in FE and HE for more than twenty years. In 2003, she sought to find progression opportunities for early years practitioners and was at the forefront of developing and directing the FD and BA Early Childhood Studies at Middlesex University. She is currently Associate Professor of Early Childhood Studies and Education and holds a BA Hons Sociology, an MSc Rights in Education and a PG Cert HE and in Counselling. Her life focus is social justice for disadvantaged groups and her doctoral research focus is on equipping students to empower families and to support children's emotional well-being.

Jacqueline Harding is a former head teacher, government consultant and BBC Education Editor. She is interested in child development in relation to media and how the definition of literacy is expanding. Jacqueline writes extensively on the subject of media and child development. Throughout her work she has sought to better understand how media can enhance children's social and emotional development and enrich their learning experiences. She is currently a Senior Lecturer at Middlesex University.

Margrethe Jernes is a qualified researcher with a PhD in Educational Sciences. Her thesis concerned interaction in digital contexts in Early Childhood Education (ECE). She also teaches adult students on early years teacher training programmes. Her interest is teaching and learning in ECE, specialising in digital technology. In addition, she has an interest in adult learning and supervision as for the last eighteen years she has been teaching at university on various further education and MA programmes. Her current position is Associate Professor at the Department of Early Childhood Education at the University of Stavanger in Norway.

Lorraine Kaye is a qualified primary teacher with an MA in Teaching and a BEd (Hons) with a specialism in computer education. She is committed to the use of technology in education as a tool to both improve teaching and learning and to motivate and excite learners. Throughout her career she has worked with a wide range of audiences including schools, colleges, ITT education bodies, government departments, technical staff, young people, parents and colleagues. For the last twelve years she has taught students on undergraduate and postgraduate primary and early years teacher training programmes. She is currently the subject leader for computing in primary and early years education for Middlesex University.

Angela Scollan joined Middlesex University in 2012 as Senior Lecturer in Early Childhood Studies, Education and Early Years Initial Teacher Training. She was previously a lecturer of Early Childhood Studies at Roehampton University, director of a bespoke early years and education training company, a freelance Ofsted inspector and EYPS lead assessor. Angela also taught and managed foundation degrees for six years at Carshalton College in Surrey. Previously, she worked within the early years sector in a variety of teaching and practitioner roles where her passion for children's rights, self-determination, emotional intelligence, play and reflexivity grew and were impacted upon directly during interactions with children, families and peers. Her areas of interest in teaching and research are: children's rights; reflective and critical thinking; professional identity and progression; Forest School and outside learning environments; ethical practice; assessment, study skills and academic transition programmes.

Nicky Spawls is Senior Lecturer and Director of Programmes for the BA Education Studies, BA Early Childhood Studies and EYTS at Middlesex University. Nicky has over twenty years' experience in adult education primarily in the fields of developmental psychology, and health and education. With a BA in Psychology and Anthropology, and an MA in Medical Anthropology, Nicky now focuses her research and teaching on her combined interests of anthropology and child development.

Dilys Wilson started her career as a nursery/Infant teacher and spent many years in further education training for early years practitioners. She is currently Programme Leader for Early Years Initial Teacher Training (EYITT) at Middlesex University. Working with young children and training early years practitioners has enabled her to pursue her interest in the social and emotional factors involved in the process of learning. She is particularly interested in early development and learning environments for children under three and the role of parents and practitioners in supporting education and care practices.

Introduction

Young children today are living in a world in which they constantly encounter digital technologies; at home, in the environment, in pre-school and beyond. It is widely accepted that we are in the midst of a digital revolution, an ongoing process of social, political, and economic change brought about by digital technology, such as computers and the internet. Increased global connectivity and the use of the internet in the UK and beyond has greatly influenced the world in which young children live. Children's experiences with technology will therefore have significant implications for their future lives. Recent research by Plowman *et al.* supports the importance of providing children with the skills that they will need to operate in a technological age:

> One response to the question of whether it is important that young children learn to use digital media is a pragmatic one: we live in a technological age so it follows that children need the skills, competences and enthusiasms to function and flourish in the world in which they are growing up.
>
> (Plowman *et al.*, 2012)

While there are a number of books with ideas for using technology with early years – for example Trythall (2007) and Siraj-Blatchford and Morgan (2009) – there are fewer which address the pedagogy relating to their use. I realised this when my early years students struggled to find books or journals in this area for an assignment for their technology module. This book examines the issues from a pedagogical standpoint, highlighting the importance of young children's experiences in early years education reflecting the world in which they operate. It will consider established theories of learning and development alongside findings emerging from research across the disciplines of neuroscience, psychology and education. The book also addresses social and cultural factors including the consideration of children's learning in a digital age, developments in the computing curriculum brought about by a societal workforce need; equality of access to computing, including the internet, and appropriate digital equipment at home and at school; cultural factors and access; addressing e-safety issues, supporting children to be safe and responsible users. A recurring theme explores and discusses the pedagogical shift for early years teachers and the importance of parental attitudes and involvement. There are also suggested areas for discussion and reflection at the end of each chapter on the issues they focus on.

Contributors to this book come from a variety of backgrounds but all have considerable experience within early years education. Each has drawn on their experience to address the issues from their perspective and with reference to relevant research in their field. A number of the chapters demonstrate effective collaboration between members of the Early Education team at Middlesex University in contributing their ideas and research for the advancement of knowledge and understanding of young children's learning and development.

There continues to be much debate about the impact of the increased access to technology on young children's health and well-being. There are those who see technology as responsible for children's lack of social skills and emotional development (Plowman *et al.*, 2010). They feel that technology has adverse effects on pre-school children because they are still developing cognitively and socially and early exposure to television or computers will have harmful effects (American Academy of Pediatrics, 2010).

However, other studies increasingly suggest that toddlers learn from screens when they are interactive. Current research further indicates that toddlers 'are more likely to demonstrate learning from video when interacting with a contingently responsive social partner on screen' (Kirkorian and Pempek, 2013).

The point is not so much that children are using the internet and mobile technologies in their daily lives; rather, the point is that to learn, engage, participate, play, work or socialise, children already do and will increasingly rely upon ICT (Livingstone and Bulger, 2013). It is, therefore, neither possible nor beneficial to consider preventing young children's use of technology in this information age.

Lorraine Kaye, November 2015

References

American Academy of Pediatrics (AAP) (2010). Policy statement—Media education. *Pediatrics*, 126(5): 1012–17. www.pediatrics.org/cgi/doi/10.1542/peds.2010-1636 (accessed 17 September 2015).

Kirkorian, H. L. and Pempek, T. A. (2013). Toddlers and touch screens: Potential for early learning? *Zero to Three Journal*, 33: 32–33.

Livingstone, S. and Bulger, M. E. (2013). A global agenda for children's rights in the digital age: Recommendations for developing UNICEF's research strategy. Florence: UNICEF. Retrieved from www.unicef-irc.org/publications/702 (accessed 30 March 2016).

Plowman, L., Stephen, C. and McPake, J. (2010). Supporting young children's learning with technology at home and in preschool. *Research Papers in Education*, 25(1): 93–113.

Plowman, L., McPake, J. and Stephen, C. (2012). Extending opportunities for learning: The role of digital media in early education. In S. Suggate and E. Reese (eds) *Contemporary Debates in Child Development and Education*. Abingdon: Routledge, pp. 95–104.

Siraj-Blatchford, J. and Morgan, A. (2009). *Using ICT in the Early Years*. London: Step Forward Publishing.

Trythall, A. (2007). *The Little Book of ICT*. London: Featherstone Education.

1

Young children in a digital age

Lorraine Kaye

Introduction

This chapter will consider developments in technology, particularly mobile and touchscreen technology, and how they impact on children's lives and the implications for teaching and learning in the early years. Particular reference is made to how technology supports constructivist learning theory. According to a constructivism paradigm, learning is an active process where children construct meaning out of the information being presented (Oluwafisayo, 2010). The relationship between sociocultural context and the use of technology in the early years will also be considered.

Developments in technology

The rate at which technology develops is exponential. The ability to produce more powerful and faster processors for use in smaller and more affordable devices has led to the proliferation of smartphones, tablet computers and other ultra-portable devices, which are all becoming a part of everyday life. This is due, in part, to global developments in connectivity to the internet through broadband and wireless networks.

Recent statistics (Office for National Statistics, 2014) show that 21 million households in Great Britain had an internet connection, which represents 83 per cent of households, up from 80 per cent in 2012. The statistics indicate that internet access varies depending on household composition, with almost all households with children having an internet connection (97 per cent).

The UK's first 4G mobile network was launched in October 2012 offering faster access anywhere and it continues to expand rapidly. Recent developments have not only been limited to mobile broadband, with the availability of wireless broadband (wifi) hotspots increasing at a rapid rate. The availability of both mobile broadband and wifi networks means the mobile internet is now used by more people than ever before and the way households connect to the internet has changed considerably in recent years. Dial-up internet has almost entirely disappeared from Great Britain's internet map, with less than 1 per cent of households still connecting this way.

Touchscreen technology

Alongside the development of the speed and ease of internet access has been the development of more accessible and more mobile devices. As the use of mobile phones with internet access has grown, a myriad of features and applications have also been developed to meet demand and harness the availability of the broader range of connectivity options outlined above. The smaller screen size of earlier mobile phones made some of the text quite difficult to read and/or it was necessary to keep scrolling the text using a keypad in order to access information. The rapid advancement of touchscreen technology in the 2000s enabled easier and faster access to the information on the screen. In 2007 Steve Jobs demonstrated the first swipe-to-scroll iPhone, which has led to the development of a plethora of 'smart' devices: 'Generally speaking, if a machine/artefact does something that we think an intelligent person can do, we consider the machine to be smart' (Walter Derzko, n.d.). Smartphones and other smart devices now offer instant messaging, sending and receiving of email, satellite navigation, productivity applications (word processing, etc.) and games among the huge range of applications available.

Although more mobile computer devices were available from the late 1990s in the form of tablet devices, where the screen sat on top or swivelled around a smaller keyboard, the developments in mobile phone and touchscreen technology have led to a new generation of tablet devices. These are thinner and lighter and it is predicted that tablet sales will exceed traditional personal computer (desktops, notebooks) sales in 2015 (Gartner Inc., 2014).

Young children's access to the internet

In the UK, eight in ten children aged three to four live in a household with access to the internet through a PC, laptop or netbook (see Figure 1.1 below). Two-thirds of children aged three to four (65 per cent) live in a household with a tablet computer in the home, an increase since 2013 (from 51 per cent) (Ofcom, 2014).

The recent inclusion of children aged three to four years in the Ofcom statistics above, reflects the growth in the number of pre-school children using these devices to go online. They and most babies under the age of two in developed countries now have an online presence (or digital footprint). It could be argued that some may have a digital 'footprint' even before they are born (see Figure 1.2).

Younger children who go online at home, in particular, are five times more likely than in 2012 to use a tablet computer; and one in eight three- to four-year-olds use a tablet computer to go online (12 per cent). Games are the most commonly mentioned online activity carried out at least weekly by the majority of three- to four-year-olds (58 per cent). One-quarter of this age group watch TV at home using an alternative device, and 20 per cent use on-demand services. One in seven parents of three- to four-year-olds feel their child knows more about the internet than they do (Ofcom, 2014).

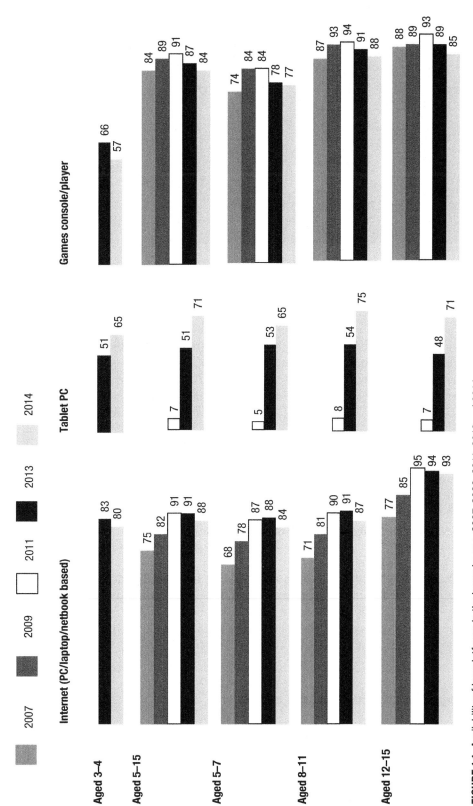

FIGURE 1.1 Availability of key platforms in the home by age: 2007, 2009, 2011, 2013 and 2014.
Source: Ofcom research; fieldwork carried out by Saville Rossiter-Base in April to June 2014.

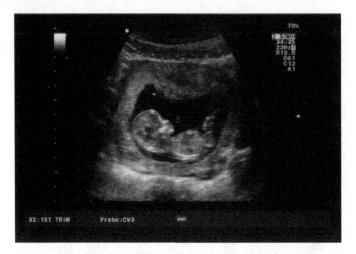

FIGURE 1.2 Scan of my unborn grandson, downloaded from Facebook.

Within Europe, between 50 per cent (Germany) and 78 per cent (Netherlands) of pre-school children access the internet. This is also reflected in other developed countries. For example, in South Korea 93 per cent of three- to nine-year-olds go online for an average of eight to nine hours a week (Jie, 2012). In the US, 25 per cent of three-year-olds go online daily, rising to about 50 per cent by age five and nearly 70 per cent by age eight (Gutnick *et al.*, 2011). In Australia, 79 per cent of children aged between five and eight years go online at home (Australian Bureau of Statistics, 2012; Holloway *et al.*, 2013). In some developing countries, large numbers of learners are moving directly to mobile devices, bypassing the personal computer stage.

More recently, smaller tablets, such as the mini iPad have appeared on the market while the screens of newer smartphones have increased in size. This has led to the development of 'phablets'. These are smartphone–tablet hybrids, with screen sizes between five and six inches, that offer the portability and functionality of a smartphone crossed with the larger touchscreen experience of a tablet. It has been suggested that 'phablets could become the dominant computing device of the future – the most popular kind of phone on the market, and perhaps the only computer many of us need' (Manjoo, 2014).

Therefore, developments in technology have seen the explosion of a multitude of other digital media including games consoles, e-readers and televisions; and touchscreen technology has become part of our everyday lives: 'Once a futuristic novelty, it's now expected in everything from music players to printers, train ticket machines to supermarket self-checkouts' (*The Guardian*, 2015).

A digital age: Social and cultural contexts

Socialisation and environment each have a large impact on how one thinks about, interacts with, and views the world. This ... requires us, as educators, to respond to the current techno–social conditions that our students experience.

(Poore, 2013)

FIGURE 1.3 A child's digital environment.

The prevalence of digital media in children's lives (see Figure 1.3) has led to a change in the way in which children engage with technology. Children (and adults) of all ages are spending an increasing number of hours per week in front of different kinds of digital media which they can control and interact with in an instinctive way, and usually through the use of touchscreens.

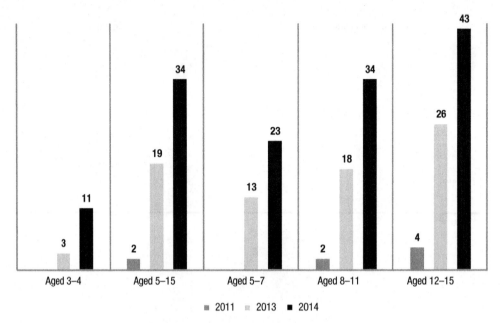

FIGURE 1.4 Tablet access, use and ownership, by age of child, 2011, 2013.
Source: Ofcom research; fieldwork carried out by Saville Rossiter-Base in April to June 2014.

Access to a tablet computer in the home in the UK has more than doubled since 2012, with this increase seen for all age groups of children and for all socio-economic groups. (see Figure 1.4 above). These statistics are backed up by qualitative evidence and anecdotal experiences. For example, a father recently told me that his three sons, aged five, seven and ten years, each have their own tablets and use them to play games with each other or to discover information on the internet. 'When the little one cannot keep up, he simply uses the voice recognition feature to access the information that the other two search for.' He explained that the children often sat in different rooms with their devices playing games against each other.

Sociocultural theory

Sociocultural theory asserts that children acquire and master the cultural tools of their situations (Göncü and Gaskins, 2011). Effective modelling and scaffolding of the meaningful use of tools provides opportunities for children to practise and hone their skills. 'This seems to be what is happening in families and so an infant who is able to unlock an iPhone™ or a toddler who turns on a computer to access an online game should be seen as participating in viable cultural activity' (Edwards, 2013).

A recent study from Stirling University's School of Education found that the family's attitude to technology at home is an important factor in influencing a child's relationship with it. The study concludes:

> The experiences of three to five-year-olds are mediated by each family's distinct sociocultural context and each child's preferences. The technology did not

dominate or drive the children's experiences; rather their desires and their family culture shaped their forms of engagement.

(Adey *et al.*, 2013)

Research by Plowman *et al.* (2012) also suggests that adults and other more able partners, such as older siblings, have a critical role in developing children's learning with computers and other digital media. This can be by showing children how to use a device or by showing interest, asking questions, making suggestions or just being there. Adults may also be unaware that their own use of digital media provides support as children learn by watching and copying. The term used to describe these various ways of providing support for learning with technology is 'guided interaction'.

Plowman *et al.* (2012) further suggest how interactions with technologies could support four main areas of learning at home:

- *Operational learning* – learning how to control and use technologies, getting them to do the things you want them to do and having opportunities to make your own inputs and get a personalised response.
- *Extending knowledge and understanding of the world* – by finding out about people, places and the natural world.
- *Dispositions to learn* – as they become increasingly competent users of digital media, children show greater concentration and persistence and their self-confidence and self-esteem flourishes.
- *The role of technology in everyday life* – as they observe adults involved in a wide range of pursuits children learn that technology provides opportunities to design things, order goods, research travel and send text messages, even though they themselves cannot yet undertake these activities.

Access to technology

In households where this technology is accessible, children under five years old appear able to use smartphones, tablet computers and games consoles almost intuitively, swiping screens and confidently pressing buttons, something I have witnessed with my four-year-old grandson. 'Even in low technology households, the home often provides a richer mix of technologies than many pre-school settings as well as providing opportunities for children both to observe and to participate in authentic activities' (Plowman *et al.*, 2010).

Therefore, young children will arrive at early years settings with varying degrees of understanding of how to operate digital technologies; many of them are able to access, manipulate and interact with a range of websites and applications. However, just as there is a concern about the differences in access to print media for children from a range of differing social, economic and cultural backgrounds, there are now similar concerns with regard to access to digital technologies (National Association for the Education of Young Children [NAEYC], 2012). Children growing up in affluent families usually have more access to technology tools and broadband connections to the internet in their homes, begin using the internet at an early age, and have highly developed technology skills and emergent digital literacy when they enter school. By contrast, children in families with fewer resources may have little or no access to the latest technologies in their homes, early childhood settings, schools or communities (NAEYC, 2012).

The Internet Access Quarterly Update (May 2014) from the Office for National Statistics reveals that while internet use is well-established and growing fast, the 'digital divide' remains a problem. According to the report, 5 per cent of households have no access to the internet, digital TV or mobile phones. This 'digital divide' is linked to household income – nine out of ten of the richest 10 per cent of households have internet access, while for the poorest 10 per cent of households only one-fifth have internet access. It is important for early years settings to be aware of this divide and provide opportunities to redress the balance.

Constructivism

Constructivism is a theory of learning developed by Piaget, Vygotsky and Bruner. Piaget believed that humans learn through the construction of one logical structure after another. He also concluded that the logic of children and their modes of thinking are initially entirely different from those of adults. The implications of this theory and how he applied them have shaped the foundation for constructivist education. Influenced by Piaget's (1896–1980) research on child development, Bruner (1973) proposed a cognitive development theory that emphasises the student's active role in the learning process. In other words, the learner formulates hypotheses, constructs new ideas, and selects information that is integrated into existing knowledge and experience. Bruner advocates teaching activities that allow students to discover and construct knowledge. Vygotsky (1978) introduced the social aspect of learning into constructivism. He defined the 'zone of proximal development' (ZPD), according to which students solve problems beyond their actual developmental level (but within their level of potential development) under adult guidance or in collaboration with more capable peers. The role of technology in young children's lives is largely perceived in terms of constructivism, exemplified by the highly influential work by Seymour Papert (1980) in using computers to teach children mathematics through his LOGO programming language.

Constructivism and technology

There are a number of researchers who have considered how constructivism can be used within technology-supported learning environments. Cunningham *et al.* (1993) formulated a set of pedagogical maxims for designers of constructivist learning environments. These include:

- All knowledge is constructed. All learning is a process of construction.
- Many worldviews can be constructed, hence there will be multiple perspectives.
- Knowledge is context dependent, so learning should occur in contexts to which it is relevant.
- Learning is mediated by tools and signs.

- Learning is inherently social–dialogical activity.
- Learners are distributed, multi-dimensional participants in a socio-cultural process.
- Knowing how we know is the ultimate human accomplishment.

(Page-Bucci, 2002)

In terms of young children's learning through constructivism, these could be translated as follows. A child learns:

- actively, not passively;
- by constructing understandings in his/her own mind;
- by building on what s/he already knows;
- when solving problems with the right level of challenge;
- through interaction.

These themes will be explored further in the final section of this chapter, which describes how they relate to the use of technology.

Implications for teaching and learning in early years

Technology is a significant part of everyday life. Most young children will have spent their entire lives surrounded by and using computers, video games, digital music players, video cams, cell phones, and all the other toys and tools of the digital age (Prensky, 2001). There is an expectation that they will have access to these technological tools in their pre-school setting.

Why use technology?

Technology is about more than supporting traditional ways of learning. It provides new ways of engaging children; new shared resources for representing things differently and for scaffolding children's thinking. Technology can enhance children's learning by:

- allowing children to engage positively in imaginative, active learning;
- offering instant feedback to children in a variety of forms;
- motivating and encouraging children to persist and take next steps;
- presenting ideas in dynamic and stimulating ways;
- providing resources for adults to use with children in their learning.

From a social constructivist view, Oluwafisayo (2010) explains that learning is seen as an active process where children construct meaning out of the information being presented. He also highlights the point that learning is a social activity and children learn well from interaction and conversation with their peers and teachers. As stated by Berryman (1994), 'one aspect of constructivism is the social collaboration that takes place. Collaboration is key in applying constructivist principles, whether the collaboration takes place between teacher and student, or student to student'. The teacher provides the scaffolding and support for students to acquire the appropriate skill and the child contributes their thinking and development knowledge. A study conducted by Parette *et al.* (2009) noted that education professionals were missing opportunities to use technology to embrace a developmentally appropriate practice. 'Our society has become dependent on technology in virtually all aspects of modern day life, yet early childhood settings still lag substantively behind in embracing the potential of a vast cadre of new and powerful learning tools' (Parette *et al.*, 2009). Children are often left to their own devices; the technology may be made available but there is little interaction with practitioners (see Chapter 6).

The integration of technology into early childhood programmes

Integration of technology and media into early childhood programmes involves the use of resources such as computers, digital cameras, software applications, and the internet in daily classroom practices (Edutopia, 2007). True integration occurs when the use of technology and media becomes routine and transparent – when the focus of a child or educator is on the activity or exploration itself and not on the technology or media being used as advocated by constructivist theory. Technology integration has been successful when the use of technology and media supports the goals of educators and programs for children, provides children with digital tools for learning and communicating, and helps improve child outcomes (Edutopia, 2007). See also Chapter 5.

Effective teaching and learning with technology

The use of technology can make learning and teaching more effective through the use of interactive resources which develop children's thinking and this is explored in more depth in a number of other chapters. It is also a motivational tool engaging children across areas of learning and give opportunities for practice and reinforcement. Additionally, it encourages social interaction and develops children's language skills (see Chapter 3). Children should have the opportunity to explore technological applications, as technology can empower young children in that it can support all learners in an inclusive way and enable better access to the curriculum for all children. Technology then, allows children to progress at their own pace according to their own strengths, interests and learning styles.

For children with special needs, technology is especially beneficial. It can provide support for cognitive processing or enhancing memory and recall. The variety of adaptive and assistive technologies ranges from low-tech toys with simple switches to expansive high-tech systems capable of managing complex environments. These technologies have the capability to empower young children, increasing their independence and supporting their inclusion in classes with their peers. With adapted materials, young children with disabilities can be included in activities in which they once would have been unable to participate. 'By using assistive technology, educators can increase the likelihood that children will have the ability to learn, move, communicate, and create' (NAEYC, 2012). However, it is vital that all early childhood teachers understand and are able to use any assistive technologies that are available to children with special needs.

Technology supporting home–school relationships

In terms of early years provision, technology can strengthen home–school links and the relationship with the community by building relationships, maintaining ongoing communication, as well as providing the opportunity to exchange information and share online resources. Parents and families can use technology to ask questions, seek advice, share information about their child, and feel more engaged in their child's experiences. Many early childhood centres and pre-schools have developed websites and/or blogs detailing their mission, events, celebrations, initiatives and learning, for example Gamesley Early Excellence Centre (www.gamesleyeec.org.uk). Video-conferencing programs such as Skype, FaceTime and Google+ Hangouts can provide opportunities to invite parents and guests into early childhood classrooms without them having to be physically present in the classroom. This is particularly important for small and remote communities.

Using touchscreen and tablet technology in early childhood education

Clearly, much depends on the technology available to the early years professional in their setting. The design of the computer has changed very little in the last few years other than in terms of faster and more powerful processors. The use of traditional keyboard-based devices such as a computer or laptop requires a certain level of physical and motor development to use a keyboard and/or a mouse/track pad. Additionally, the use of these devices also requires a level of cognitive development to understand the symbols on the keyboard and screen. Therefore, a young child needs to be able to decode these symbols in order to engage with the device. This presents a challenge for young children who are developing their literacy skills and are likely not to have the level of reading and writing needed. The developments, outlined earlier in this chapter, of tablet/touchscreen technology in a variety of sizes, from interactive whiteboards to tablets and phablets, enables very young children to engage with these devices much more easily. The device asks for an action (touch) and the child makes a cognitive decision and acts by touching a selection. The child does not have to manipulate a mouse around a screen or decipher a keyboard to enter commands. The child simply interacts in a very natural and developmentally appropriate way with the device (Geist, 2012). 'Touch technology follows the same logic as shaking a rattle or knocking down a pile of blocks: the child swipes, and something immediately happens' (Rosin, 2013). A number of studies have been undertaken relating to the use of touchscreen devices by young children (Dezuanni et al., 2015; Henderson and Yeow, 2012; Couse and Chen, 2010) with similar results. The following study undertaken by Geist (2012) is typical of the findings.

RESEARCH STUDY

Geist (2012) found the following:

- As early as the age of two, children easily and naturally interact with the touchscreen interface in a way that is different from a traditional computer.
- Teachers in classrooms needed to provide little instruction for the two-year-old children to begin actively using the iPads in a productive manner.
- Children's ability to work and explore independently with the device is much greater than with traditional computers. Because the interface is so intuitive, using the device resembles how children play with other developmentally appropriate toys.
- The interactions with the iPad resemble more the way that children of the same age play with blocks, in a manipulative way or in a sensory table. Students interact and explore the many things that they can do on the devices and the devices respond to their efforts.
- After just one session of using the iPads, the children began to overcome their natural instinct to touch and hold the buttons and learned the appropriate 'tap' required to navigate the device. Once they achieved this, they were able to explore in a way that would not be possible on a traditional computer.
- After two sessions interacting with the iPads, the children were able to quickly becoming experts at using the devices. They could adjust the device and navigate to find the applications that they wanted. This gave the children the independence to explore the iPad and the applications that were installed on it.

What the iPad offered in this study was a vehicle for the children to demonstrate their abilities to their teachers and their parents. The degree of interactivity and independence with the devices was truly amazing, but only because the iPad was able to support the natural curiosity of the toddlers in the study.

In much of the research it was found that the interface of touchscreen tablets is intuitive so that little or no instruction is needed for even the youngest children to use them in a productive manner. Being productive on any device means that the child understands what is asked of them, understands how to interface with the device and understands the action needed to produce a response from the device (Couse and Chen, 2010).

Tablet devices therefore appear to be an effective tool for use with pre-school children. It provides early childhood teachers with another tool for implementing technology standards and curriculum to prepare children to be digital citizens who are technologically literate (Couse and Chen, 2010). This is evident when you look at the development of content (apps) for mobile devices. According to a January 2012 analysis of the education category in Apple's App Store conducted by the Joan Ganz Cooney Center, nearly three-quarters of the top-selling apps targeted pre-school- or elementary-age children, and the most popular were 'early learning apps' aimed at toddlers and pre-schoolers (Adey *et al.*, 2013). However, recent research highlights the significance of utilising a tablet device such as an iPad to advance effective pedagogy, rather than solely concentrating on the software opportunities they provide (Andrews, 2013). Consequently, an emphasis has been placed on the training that teachers receive on how to harness and utilise the full capabilities of iPads (Karsenti and Fievez, 2013).

In a recent paper, Edwards considers:

> [I]n a more digitally mediated era, what should we offer those children who come to the early years classroom understanding how to operate touchscreen technologies and heading towards needing to be able to take, manipulate and share digital imagery? Should we be paying more attention to the range of apps that let pre-schoolers create, narrate and store digital stories? Should we be thinking more carefully about how children's media inspired play is being recognised in the home as a site for learning? Perhaps mobile technologies need to be as freely available and common as the use of blocks in the block corner?
>
> (Edwards, 2013)

Modern technologies and mobile devices such as iPads and document cameras are quickly becoming valuable tools to engage children, support assessment, and enhance communication. Fleer (2013) examined the many benefits of tablet devices such as the iPad in early years, taking a different approach by focusing on its use by teachers with regard to the assessment opportunities that it provides. Fleer points out that the use of the iPad for assessment by teachers can be advantageous as it allows them to document children's learning instantaneously via photos and sound recordings. The teacher can then revisit this learning later and add comments before uploading. The school in Fleer's study bought into an assessment program using iPads and an assessment application. As educators explore these new technologies as tools to support learning, they are also experiencing and implementing the potential opportunities technology can provide to complete assessments as well as also sharing achievements, observation and learning with parents simultaneously (see Chapter 6).

A recent Horizon report on emerging technology in education (Johnson et al., 2012) suggests that tablet computing was one of *the* hot trends for technology adoption in schools in 2013, alongside mobile devices and apps. There is evidence of increased adoption of tablet devices and other 'post-PC' tablets in schools around the world (Johnson et al., 2012; Quillan, 2011; Henderson and Yeow, 2012) as well as in the UK (BESA, 2012; Heinrich, 2012). However, the adoption and integration of tablet devices into school systems has not been without its controversies, be they pedagogic, technical, political, social or economic, and these themes are considered in the following chapters.

DISCUSSION TOPICS

- What are the positive (and negative) effects of the digital revolution on young children's lives?
- How can the use of touchscreen technology and the increased use of mobile technology (tablets, smartphones, for example) impact on teaching and learning in early years?
- Consider the ways a child's home access to technology could impact on their learning.

Conclusion

Young children live in a world where digital technologies are pervasive. Children under five years old appear able to use smartphones, tablet computers and games consoles almost intuitively and research indicates that this pattern will certainly continue in the future (NAEYC, 2012). It is not possible to predict what developments there might be in the future: 'we are preparing students for jobs that don't yet exist, using technologies that haven't yet been invented, in order to solve problems we don't even know are problems yet' (Fisch, 2008).

ANECDOTES OF YOUNG CHILDREN'S INTERACTION WITH TECHNOLOGY

When my granddaughter turned three I made the mistake of giving her a toy mobile phone for her birthday. She excitedly opened the present, but was obviously disappointed when I showed her that we could only have pretend telephone conversations. Examining the toy phone carefully, she then looked at me sympathetically, explaining, 'They should have given you a sim card when you got this – they don't work without sim cards, Nanny'.

(Puerling, n.d.)

I had been reading a picture book on my smartphone with my eighteen-month-old granddaughter and she was helping by swiping the pages. I then picked up one of her picture books and she looked puzzled when she could not 'swipe' the pages of the book to turn them. She looked at her finger quizzically and said 'not working'.

(Peter, 2015)

Parents and practitioners are aware that there is a balance in supporting children's learning and development in a digital age and that they need to consider new and, perhaps unfamiliar, strategies for teaching and learning with technology in early years. Young children have had a very different upbringing in terms of their relationships with screen and texts to those of previous generations and certainly my students think I must be extremely old when I tell them that when I was young, television consisted of one channel and was only on for a few hours a day. Pre-school children today have a very different attitude to technology and accept technological gadgets as part of their environment. Certainly, the technological skills that children need to develop to function in a digital age did not exist when many present-day teachers were pre-schoolers. It could be argued that the rapid developments in touchscreen and voice-activated technology may mean that some of the skills young children are being taught, such as being able to use a mouse, may well be obsolete before they leave their primary classroom. Investment in technological resources in pre-school to foster children's digital literacy is, therefore, as important as providing any other equipment to support their learning and development.

Engaging children's natural inclination for play and discovery while ensuring they are prepared for the global economy will require urgent reform in current models of early learning. In the next decade, teachers and other educators must establish new forms of practice, enhanced and supported by the most modern and productive technology tools available.

(Barron *et al.*, 2011: 45)

References

Adey, C., Steven, C. and Stevenson, O. (2013). Young children engaging with technologies at home: The influence of family context. *Journal of Early Childhood Research,* 11(2): 149–164.

Andrews, D. (2013). iPads in Primary Education (blog): http://mrandrewsonline.blogspot.co.uk/ (accessed October 2014).

Australian Bureau of Statistics (2012). Children's internet access and mobile phone ownership, selected characteristics. Children's Participation in Cultural and Leisure Activities, Australia, April 2012. www.abs.gov.au/websitedbs/D3310114.nsf/home/home?opendocument (accessed October 2014).

Barron, B., Cayton-Hodges, G., Bofferding, L., Copple, C., Darling-Hammond, L. and Levine, M. (2011). *Take a Giant Step: A Blueprint for Teaching Children in a Digital Age.* New York: The Joan Ganz Cooney Center at Sesame Workshop.

Berryman, S. (1994). *Cognitive Science: Challenging Schools to Design Effective Learning Environments.* New York: Columbia University, Teachers College, Institute on Education and the Economy.

BESA (2012). The Future of Tablets and Apps in Schools, www.besa.org.uk/sites/default/files/tab2013_0.pdf (accessed August 2015).

Bruner, J. (1973). *Going Beyond the Information Given.* New York: Norton.

Couse, L. J. and Chen, D. W. (2010). A tablet computer for young children? Exploring its viability for early childhood education. *Journal of Research on Technology in Education,* 43(1): 75–98.

Cunningham, D., Duffy, T. M. and Knuth, R. (1993). Textbook of the future. In C. McKnight (ed.), *Hypertext: A Psychological Perspective.* London: Ellis Horwood Publishing.

Derzko, W. *Smart Technologies in The New Smart Economy.* http://smarteconomy.typepad.com/smart_economy/2007/06/smart_economy_a.html (accessed April 2015).

Dezuanni, M., Dooley, K., Gattenhof, S. and Knight, L. (2015). *IPads in the Early Years: Developing Literacy and Creativity.* Abingdon: Routledge.

Edutopia (2007). *What Is Successful Technology Integration? Well-Integrated Use of Technology Resources by Thoroughly Trained Teachers Makes Twenty-First-Century Learning Possible.* www.edutopia.org/technology-integration-guide-description (accessed August 2015).

Edwards, S. (2013). By-passing the debate: Beyond the 'technology question' in the early years. http://tactyc.org.uk/pdfs/Reflection-Edwards.pdf (accessed August 2015).

Fisch, K. (2008). *Shift Happens.* [video] Available at: www.youtube.com/watch?v=emx92kBKads (accessed May 2015).

Fleer, M. (2013). Digital positioning for inclusive practice in early childhood: The cultural practices surrounding digital tablets in family homes. *Computers in New Zealand Schools: Learning, Teaching, Technology,* 25(1–3), 56–76.

Gartner Inc. (2014). Gartner says worldwide traditional PC, tablet, ultramobile and mobile phone shipments are on pace to grow 6.9 percent in 2014. www.gartner.com/newsroom/id/2692318 (accessed October 2014).

Geist, E. A. (2012). A qualitative examination of two-year-olds interaction with tablet based interactive technology. *Journal of Instructional Psychology,* 39(1): 26–35.

Göncü, A. and Gaskins, S. (2011). Comparing and extending Piaget's and Vygotsky's understandings of play: Symbolic play as individual, sociocultural, and educational interpretation. In A. D. Pellegrini (ed.) *Oxford Handbook of the Development of Play.* Oxford: Oxford University Press.

The Guardian (15 July 2011). Pointing the way: How touchscreen technology has changed our lives. www.theguardian.com/sound-artists/touchscreen-technology-change-lives (accessed June 2015).

Gutnick, A. L., Bernstein, L. and Levine, M. H. (2011). *Always Connected: The New Digital Media Habits of Young Children*. New York: The Joan Ganz Cooney Center at Sesame Workshop. www.joanganzcooneycenter.org/publication/always-connected-the-new-digital-media-habits-of-young-children/ (accessed October 2014).

Heinrich, P. (2012). *The iPad as a Tool for Education*. NAACE and 9ine Consulting. www.naace.co.uk/get.html?_Action=GetFile&_Key=Data26613&_Id=1965&_Wizard=0&_DontCache=1341555048 (accessed August 2015).

Henderson, S. and Yeow, J. (2012). iPad in Education: A case study of iPad adoption and use in a primary school. www.computer.org/csdl/proceedings/hicss/2012/4525/00/4525a078.pdf (accessed October 2015).

Holloway, D., Green, L. and Brady, D. (2013). 0–8: Young children's internet use. Paper presented at the Australian and New Zealand Communication Association Conference, Fremantle, Australia, July 3–5, 2013.

Jie, S. H. (2012 Sep 25-7). ICT use statistics of households and individuals in Korea. Presented at 10th World Telecommunication/ICT Indicators Meeting (WTIM-12), Bangkok, Thailand, 25–27 September 2012. www.itu.int/ITU-D/ict/wtim12/documents/cont/029_E_doc.pdf (accessed October 2014).

Johnson, L., Adams, S. and Cummins, M. (2012). NMC Horizon Report: 2012 K–12 Edition. Austin, Texas: The New Media Consortium.

Karsenti, T. and Fievez, A. (2013). *The ipad in education: Uses, benefits, and challenges – A survey of 6,057 students and 302 teachers in Quebec (Canada)*. Montreal, QC: CRIFPE.

Manjoo, F. (2014). With the iPhone 6 Plus, Apple aims for versatility. *The New York Times*, 17 September 2014.

NAEYC (2012). *Technology and Interactive Media as Tools in Early Childhood Programs Serving Children from Birth through Age 8*. A joint position statement of the National Association for the Education of Young Children and the Fred Rogers Center for Early Learning and Children's Media at Saint Vincent College. www.naeyc.org/files/naeyc/file/positions/PS_technology_WEB2.pdf (accessed August 2015).

Ofcom (2014). *Children and Parents: Media Use and Attitudes Report*. http://stakeholders.ofcom.org.uk/market-data-research/other/research-publications/childrens/children-parents-oct-14/ (accessed August 2015).

Office for National Statistics (2014). *Internet Access Quarterly Update, Q1*. www.ons.gov.uk/ons/rel/rdit2/internet-access-quarterly-update/q1-2014/stb-ia-q1-2014.html (accessed August 2014).

Oluwafisayo, E. (2010). Constructivism and web 2.0 in the emerging learning era: A global perspective. *Journal of Strategic Innovation and Sustainability*, 6(4): 16–25. www.na-businesspress.com/JSIS/EnobunWeb.pdf

Page-Bucci, H. (2002). *Investigating the Characteristics of Effective Distance Learning, Computer Based Learning and Training Principles*. www.hkadesigns.co.uk/websites/msc/prin/#TABLE per cent20OF per cent20CONTENTS (accessed August 2015).

Papert, S. (1980). *Mindstorms: Children, Computers and Powerful Ideas*. New York: Basic Books.

Parette, H., Quesenberry, A. and Blum, C. (2010). Missing the boat with technology usage in early childhood settings: A 21st century view of developmentally appropriate practice. *Early Childhood Education Journal*, 37: 335–343.

Plowman, L., Stephen, C. and McPake, J. (2010). Supporting young children's learning with technology at home and in preschool. *Research Papers in Education*, 25(1): 93–113.

Plowman, L., McPake, J. and Stephen, C. (2012). Extending opportunities for learning: The role of digital media in early education. In S. Suggate and E. Reese (eds) *Contemporary Debates in Child Development and Education*. Abingdon: Routledge, pp. 95–104.

Poore, M. (2013). *Using Social Media in the Classroom*. London: Sage.

Prensky, M. (2001). Digital natives, digital immigrants. *On the Horizon*, 9(5): 1–6.

Puerling, B. (n.d.). See www.asg.co.nz/page.aspx?ID=5435 (accessed April 2015).

Quillan, I. (2011). Educators evaluate learning benefits of iPad. *Education Week*, 4(3): 38, 40–41. Available online: www.edweek.org/dd/articles/2011/06/15/03mobile.h04.html (accessed January 2014).

Rosin, H. (2013). The touchscreen generation. *The Atlantic*, 20 March 2013. www.theatlantic.com/magazine/archive/2013/04/the-touch-screen-generation/309250/4/ (accessesd August 2015).

Vygotsky, L. (1978). *Mind in Society: The Development of Higher Psychological Processes*. Cambridge, MA: Harvard University Press.

2

Why are young children so good with technology?

Nicky Spawls and Dilys Wilson

Introduction

An internet search about young children's use of the latest digital technology reveals a combination of fascination about the aptitude babies and very young children display and alarm about the possible implications for their development and well-being. Smartphones, tablet computers and games consoles have become part of young children's everyday experience and so has parental uncertainty about how to navigate their children's attraction to increasingly sophisticated but also child-friendly digital technologies (see Chapter 1). Research on the swiftly changing nature of young children's engagement with technology and the impact this could have on their development and learning is only just beginning.

Developing the capacity to think involves a combination of factors beginning with an enabling emotional and physical environment. Children learn through the interactions they have with familiar adults and other children when their curiosity is encouraged and they have opportunities to play, explore and express themselves. They also bring their unique set of family experiences and culture with them into early years care and education settings and the same is true for their familiarity with a digital world. To help shed more light on why young children are so good with technology this chapter will consider established theories of learning and development alongside findings emerging from research across the disciplines of neuroscience, psychology and education.

The contribution of neuroscience

Neuroscience has provided a complementary medical perspective to add to the substantial body of knowledge gained from educational and psychological research, confirming the connection between body and mind, physiology and psychology. Although there are many possible interpretations of the neural processes that influence behaviour and learning, research into brain development in utero and throughout early childhood has become more sophisticated through the use of neuroimaging technology. This has enabled neuroscientists to use non-invasive procedures to study human brain development and form a clearer understanding of the mechanisms underpinning the way children develop and learn (Mareschal *et al.*, 2013).

The human brain contains millions of specialised cells that keep the human body functioning. Neurons send and receive vital information to maintain life but also to control thoughts and actions. Although many of these cells are in place before birth the brain continues to lay down neural pathways throughout life in accordance with the experiences that are encountered. In this respect, babies are born with flexible brains that are responsive to whatever environment they are brought up in. This flexibility is referred to as the brain's 'plasticity'. Studies in neuroscience have indicated that both babyhood and adolescence are the most significant periods of neurological plasticity – a fact that is highly relevant in any understanding of the impact of digital technology on the developing child (Balbernie, 2001).

Greenhough (1987) suggests that the brain has different levels of plasticity: '*experience expectant plasticity*', which is the development of neural pathways in terms of expected physical processes – for example, those related to walking or toilet training that are common to all humans, and '*experience dependant plasticity*', which is unique to each individual and will develop specifically in relation to one's own experience. The brain will be adaptable to the learning of skills, development of relationships, cultural and social knowledge, and knowledge related to the implements of use in their environment.

Neuroscientists also agree that there are sensitive periods in brain development when the brain can make optimum use of experiences and environmental changes. This is particularly well-documented with reference to the development of sensory skills such as hearing and vision. Blakemore and Frith (2005: 29) discuss studies by Daphne Maurer on the timing of medical interventions to operate on babies who are born with cataracts. Delaying the operations until babies are older and when there would be less medical risk to the baby has implications for later visual perception, illustrating the importance of visual stimulation in the early months of life. How far this can be applied to the optimum timing of other early learning opportunities is an area of interest to education research and practice and is also relevant to a discussion on young children's exposure to digital technologies. On the one hand, the concept of the brain's plasticity has opened up the possibility for the effectiveness of life-long learning, but on the other, the concept of sensitive periods provides a recognition that more easily facilitated learning could take place during specific windows of development.

Babies are born ready to relate to others and they 'show a clear preference for looking at face-like patterns, rather than patterns with the same elements scrambled up, within days of birth' (Murray, 2014: 8). At birth babies also have the ability to imitate the facial movements and expressions of others. Further insight into the processes in the brain that underpin this early capacity to imitate and, as children develop, their skill in understanding the actions, intentions and feelings of others, has been provided through research on 'neural mirroring systems' (Marshall and Meltzoff, 2011).

Mirror neurons

In 1992 a team of Italian neuroscientists from the University of Parma discovered mirror neurons during their research into areas of the brain activated through the motor movements of macaque monkeys. By chance they noticed that when a monkey watched another monkey take a peanut and eat it, some of the neurons in the watching monkey's brain produced an electrical impulse which mirrored that of the monkey eating the peanut. Macaque monkeys are often used in research as they are genetically similar to humans, so the research team's findings have led to ongoing research to establish if a similar firing of mirror neurons occurs in the human brain.

These are of particular interest to educational and ideas psychological research as learning theory suggests that children learn from the actions and behaviour of others. The physiological firing of mirror neurons, which then lead to thinking and feeling associated with the observed experience from the actions and behaviours of others, provides an interesting model to explore. Returning to the question of why young children are so good with technology, could it be that they have keenly observed the use of remote controls, smartphones, tablet computers and more by the key people in their lives along with all the verbal and non-verbal expression associated with using such technology?

How babies become thinkers

It has become clear from years of research that babies are born to learn. Even from the first few minutes of life they are taking in sensory information from their surroundings and laying down neural pathways that will result in increasingly sophisticated understandings of the world. Although humans start life with a limited repertoire of abilities and limited prior knowledge, nevertheless they have an astounding capacity to learn and to modify their understanding according to their environment.

Integral to theories of cognitive development is the belief that babies are active in their learning, consciously seeking to understand the world and make sense of it. They are motivated to learn, hardwired to make sense of the jigsaw of their environments. Bransford notes how recent developments in the methods for studying the world of babies' minds has shown that, even within their simple repertoires, babies are 'able to set goals, plan and revise', 'integrating sight and sound … assembling and organising material … as they explore their perceptual worlds' (Bransford et al., 2000: 80).

According to the constructivist theory of cognitive development small babies up to the age of two are firmly within the sensori–motor stage with the majority of their thinking being focused on their physical functions, their sensory experiences and the acquisition of motor skills (Piaget, 1936). Vision, hearing and touch are primary to this stage of understanding as babies integrate information from these sensory domains to form a knowledge base of the world around them.

Language is central in this process of 'making sense of the world'. Indeed, it is well-documented that babies are drawn to language and prefer to listen to it than to other noises. If babies had to make judgements about the importance of all stimuli in their environment then their brains may well not cope, but research shows that babies attend closely only to certain types of stimuli. Language is the most salient of these (Bransford *et al.*, 2000). As infants listen in to the dialogues around them they assimilate knowledge of the world they live in and so come to make sense of it. These linguistic interactions imbibe them into their community, revealing to them their society's knowledge and understanding of the world and, as such, language will be a central feature for helping them navigate their developmental paths. Language, according to Vygotsky (1962), is the means by which adults transmit knowledge to children directly and indirectly and thus is the key to intellectual development.

The importance of adaptation

Piaget and other cognitive theorists saw that adaptation was integral to human survival. Human babies, they argued, are born with the predisposition to learn to survive in whatever environment they find themselves in, be that living in a desert region or the icy climes of the tundra. Adaptation is fundamental to human development because each person's experience is different and therefore the brain needs to be flexible enough to make sense of experiences in order to develop the necessary skills and knowledge for whichever situation humans find themselves in.

Piaget (1936) identified babies as being 'constructivist' in their approach to learning and information processing. Humans build upon their experiences, with each new concept or skill being constructed upon the previous. Piaget developed the idea of schemas as being the building blocks of learning representing how, as new information is assimilated, knowledge and skills change and develop. The environment in which babies grow is thus fundamental in determining what they learn. While it is important to acknowledge the predispositions of one's biological blueprint, it is well-established that human development occurs as a result of interactions with the environment and therefore experiences within that environment are crucial to how people develop as individuals. Babies and young children actively interact with their environments and build concepts about the world around them based on their observations of others and their own physical explorations. They go beyond imitation by building and creating new explorative possibilities of their own (Gopnik, 2009).

Bruner proposed that babies and young children go through a sequence of representation systems that enable them to develop their thinking skills. He used the term 'enactive' to explain the process of learning through real experiences and physical interaction followed by 'iconic' where visual clues remind children of their actions and consolidate past experience. 'Symbolic' refers to the means by which information is coded and stored conceptually and by representation in the mind, often through the means of language (Driscoll, 2005). As children develop and begin to make use of these approaches to learning interchangeably, they use the most effective strategy to tackle the specific learning task.

Touchscreen technology

Observe a young child working with a tablet computer and you will quickly see that they seem almost naturally predisposed to it and, when given the opportunity to play with it, they pick up the necessary skills easily and fluidly. Touchscreen technology is immediately responsive to exploring fingers and the satisfaction of having caused something to happen is similar to the experience of knocking down a pile of blocks. Adding to this sense of accomplishment, it is the same 'toy' they have seen their parents using and they have observed the level of engagement they model.

It is arguable that touchscreen technology operates on Bruner's sequence of representation systems. It is enactive by being dependent on a degree of physical control and coordination; it is iconic in that reading a screen involves making sense of iconic, visual representations, literally the 'icons' on the screen; and it is symbolic in that it includes language use and conceptual understanding to interact with it (see Chapter 4). This may, in part, explain why babies and young children are so good with touchscreen technology and why they are drawn to it.

Digital technology as a cultural tool

So where does digital technology fit in with these models of cognitive development? In Vygotsky's sociocultural theory, he suggested that children learn through social interactions with others about their society and the world through their interaction with the 'tools of culture' (Vygotsky, 1962). These 'cultural tools' refer to instruments which are central to the construction of any society. In a cross-cultural perspective the tools of a society might literally be tools such as an axe or a hoe, tools which are fundamental to that society's daily cultural life. They might also be metaphysical tools such as the language that is used; the terms and expressions which represent cultural ideas, the ethos, values and concerns of that specific social group at that moment in time. For many societies the pen and paper are essential cultural tools by which ideas are represented symbolically through the written form and literacy is a necessary skill for survival. Recent changes in the nature of the modern environment mean that digital technology has arguably become a central cultural tool. The skills needed to use these cultural tools could be considered fundamental to everyday life in many parts of the world. The requisite knowledge and information for interacting with technology are part of the construction of a global knowledge, even to the degree that their accessibility and speed informs cultural expectations.

Social cultural theorists, Vygotsky among them, have postulated that most learning takes place in the context of relationships 'between people, contexts, actions, meanings, communities, and cultural histories as well as cultural tools and artefacts' (Robbins 2005: 142). It is the dialogue, actions and interactions with others that will inform young learners of what it is they need to know. The importance here is the emphasis on social interactions as the mediator for much of this knowledge. The tools are the conduit but the essence of the ideas is largely transmitted verbally and it is important to recognise this fact in any discussion about how babies learn and the role of technology in their learning. Sociocultural theory highlights the fundamentally collaborative nature of cognitive development and is an issue that has been researched in depth by Barbara Rogoff. According to Rogoff, cognition and the development of understanding takes place 'through a collaborative process that is intrinsically related to participation with others in socioculturally relevant activities' (Robbins, 2005: 143).

It is inevitable then that children are going to need to engage with such tools as their learning and understanding of the modern world has become dependent on interactions with these tools. But what is also clear is that it is the way that parents, adults and peers support them in their negotiations with such technology that will determine the type and degree of influence that it will have in their lives and development.

A parent describes how a holiday trip to Portugal demonstrated the dependence and value of using a smartphone:

> I noticed whilst we were travelling that the smartphone I was using was central in everything we were doing. We used the sat-nav to help us find the apartment, we were listening to music whilst we travelled, we read the newspaper online, we gave it to the children to play games when we needed to manage a long and arduous journey, we gave it to the baby to watch a show we had downloaded on iPlayer when the older kids were busy and I checked in on my e-mails on occasions so that I did not lose touch with my business while I was away.

Observing their multitude of uses in their parents' lives, plus the brightly coloured engaging visual appearance of the touchscreen device, it is little wonder then that babies and young children are drawn to such gadgets. These are the cultural tools of their generation – highly visible in modern society and offering access to a wealth of information.

Relationships and their role in learning

One of the key features influencing the learning of babies and young children is the social and emotional environment in which they grow. Warm and loving relationships with key individuals have long been recognised as playing a fundamental role in children's developmental outcomes. Stemming from the work of John Bowlby in the 1950s, attachment theory has come a long way and been through a range of modifications, but the basic principle remains the same – for optimum psychological and emotional development children need to be raised in a responsive social environment of unconditional love and warmth. Indeed, attachment research has continued to preoccupy a considerable amount of research and has extended to an understanding of the way in which social relationships feed into cognitive development, self-efficacy and learning predispositions (Bandura, 1997; Goldberg, 2000).

More recent studies have gone further to propose that a baby's social and emotional environment will influence their neurological makeup. Balbernie (2001: 238) suggests that '[t]he caregiving environment has a specific impact on the infant's maturing brain as it is automatically creating neural circuits that mirror his experiences'. Emotional communication between babies and caregivers contributes to brain development and while it is well-established that negative early experiences such as abuse and neglect may lead to a range of developmental problems including developmental delay and learning disabilities, the converse also is true (Seigal, 1999; Schore, 2001).

Research study

Research by Wooldridge and Shapka (2012) suggests that fewer turn-taking conversations take place between parents and toddlers when they are playing with electronic toys in contrast to play with non-electronic toys. They also highlight that children respond less to electronic voices and are more likely to require prompts before they do so. Lerner and Barr (2014: 4) advise that 'although there is not a reliable body of research yet on the use of touchscreens, the early findings suggest that there are positive effects when parents actively participate and make screen use an interactive experience'.

However, as digital technologies advance and opportunities for young children to 'play' with digital technology and electronic toys increase, how will this impact on young children's experience? For example, recent media reports about an interactive 'smart' Barbie doll (Gibbs, 2015) which can have conversations with a child and develop a set of personalised responses through voice recognition technology, raise a number of ethical issues and concerns about children's social and emotional well-being.

Self-regulation

Self-regulation has come to be understood as a significant tool in children's emotional and cognitive development leading to a successful predisposition to learning (Bandura, 1997; Bransford et al., 2000). Self-regulation includes the ability to 'orchestrate one's learning, to plan, monitor success and correct errors when appropriate' – all factors that play a role in effective learning (Bransford et al., 2000: 85).

Gerhardt (2004) provides a clear explanation of the impact of close relationships and responsive adults on the establishment of neural connections in a baby's brain. She discusses how early attachment behaviours carried out between a loving responsive caregiver and their child lead to the development of self-regulation. She describes how early caregiving, whereby a parent modulates their infant's well-being as they respond to their physical and emotional needs, are the seeds of later self-regulation in the child. The parent is a model for self-regulation as they modify the environment according to their baby's needs – feeding them when they are hungry, changing their clothes in response to variations in temperature, stimulating them when they are bored and rocking them to sleep when they are tired. Such regulation combined with a dialogue from the parent as they meet their baby's physical, psychological and emotional needs become an internalised dialogue within the child who will later use these very experiences to regulate themselves with a similar internal dialogue. This parental mediation of the environment plays a significant role in children's later learning strategies and metacognition.

These early experiences of being understood and of having feelings and meaning regulated by a caring and attuned adult enable babies to develop 'self-regulation' which contributes to the way they begin to process their own thinking and learning as they develop.

Thinking about thinking

The term 'metacognition' is often used to refer to children's developing awareness of their own thinking and learning processes. As they begin to use verbal expression as the primary means of communicating with others, young children become more alert to what they need to know about in order to complete learning tasks and they are more able to think about their own thinking. Dowling (2013) in her glossary of terms describes metacognition as 'thinking about thinking and consciously using different thinking strategies to solve problems'. Alongside metacognition, self-regulation brings a more nuanced concept involving the emotional, motivational and social factors influencing thinking and learning. Experience of learning through the regulatory capacity of others from birth enables the developing child to begin to manage their own experiences and emotions. Language in itself is considered to be a tool that enables children to self-regulate by verbalising their thought processes, which in turn helps them to think. In order to cope with the challenges inherent in the learning process, self-regulation also involves learning from the feelings arising from difficult as well as positive experiences.

Recent research challenges the view that metacognition is only observable in children over eight years old (Whitebread et al., 2009; Robson, 2010; Whitebread and Pino-Pasternak, 2013). Using methodology such as video footage that considers children's non-verbal actions and play, which is then reflected on with the children themselves, shows that three- and four-year-olds are able to think about their own thinking and reflect on the strategies they used. It also appears that in their play with peers children of this age use more metacognitive regulation than when they are with an adult.

Table 2.1 uses Whitebread et al.'s 'Verbal and Nonverbal Indicators of Metacognition and Self-Regulation in 3–5 year olds' (2009: Appendix 1) to explore how the use of digital technologies can support strategies for thinking and learning.

TABLE 2.1 Indicators of self-regulation and metacognition (3–5 years)

Metacognitive knowledge		
	Description of behaviour	**Digital technology example**
Persons	Refers to own and others' strengths or difficulties in learning	Digital camera: comments on skills in photographing content and challenges of storing and retrieving photos electronically
Tasks	Makes a judgement about the level of difficulty of the tasks or rates the tasks on the basis of pre-established criteria or previous knowledge	Tablet app, computer or console game: understanding the game sequences based on previous play experience
Strategies	Defines, explains or teaches others how she/he has done or learned something and evaluates the effectiveness of one or more strategies used	Using Skype: selecting the icons and making a video call. Repeating previous actions, regulating the sound and communicating with others

Metacognitive regulation		
	Description of behaviour	**Example**
Planning	Sets or clarifies task demands and expectations. Decides on ways of proceeding with the task, seeking and collecting necessary resources	Accessing the internet: selecting images of media characters to print and produce in a document
Monitoring	Self-commentates and reviews progress and performance on task (keeping track of procedures currently being undertaken and those that have been done so far). Checks and/or corrects own and others' behaviours or performance, including detection of errors	Setting up a DVD: expresses procedures to go through to insert a DVD, find the right TV channel and start the programme
Control	Changes strategies as a result of previous monitoring in order to solve the task more effectively. Applies a previously learnt strategy to a new situation. Repeats a strategy in order to check the accuracy of the outcome	Making a personal avatar: uses observations from others to develop the avatar based on personal preferences. Knows how to change the settings and save the finished version
Evaluation	Reviews own learning by explaining the task and evaluates the strategies used. Rates the quality of performance. Tests the outcome or effectiveness of a strategy in achieving a goal	Using a karaoke machine: comments on personal skill on using the machine and singing the song. Improves second performance based on experience

Emotional and motivational regulation		
	Description of behaviour	**Example**
Monitoring	Expresses awareness of positive or negative emotional experience of a task and monitors own emotional reactions while being on a task	Watching a video clip of play with friends: comments on the actions and intentions and feelings. Can reflect on what was achieved and what could have led to a different outcome
Control	Controls attention and resists distraction or returns to task after momentary distraction. Self-encourages or encourages others. Persists in the face of difficulty or remains in task without help	Tablet: focuses attention on taking part in an interactive story. Is able to pause and restart the story and continue to engage with it

Young children's use of digital technologies

Table 2.1 provides some examples of the way young children demonstrate their thinking and their capacity to regulate their learning, motivation and emotional involvement through using digital technologies. McPake *et al.*'s (2013) case study research on pre-school children's use of digital technologies in their homes illustrates the extent to which young children have incorporated a wide range of 'domestic digital technology' and 'digital toys and games' into the fabric of their play and learning. They have developed the technical skills to use digital technology and are comfortable with different means of communicating narratives through symbols, images and video conversation. They are increasingly adept at creatively making links and new meaning out of a combination of play, technical knowledge and multimodal communication.

The Ofcom *Children and Parents: Media Use and Attitudes Report* (2014) notes some changes in children's media consumption with a significant increase in the access they have to tablet computers at home (see Chapter 1). This has also been confirmed by a research project on the use of digital technologies in a sample of families with children under the age of five years in four European countries, which found that 'there are a rising number of children under the age of three who have access to all digital technologies, who use computers/laptops, digital tablets and the internet' (Palaiologou, 2014: 14). Research on the impact of these changes on children's learning and development inevitably lags behind the introduction of new technologies in the home. The combination of alarm and fascination reflected in the media is a response to widely reported survey data and expresses the conflict arising from the inevitability of digital progress and change. Screen use guidelines for parents are beginning to appear based on existing research evidence which aims to dispel some of the myths about young children's use of digital technologies (Lerner and Barr, 2014; Plowman and McPake, 2013) and engage in a debate about how best to support children's development and learning in a digital world.

DISCUSSION/REFLECTION POINTS

- Will the continuous interaction with technology from birth affect how the brains of the future are wired?
- To what extent will computers be able to replicate social and emotional interaction?
- Could they facilitate human communication or will they, as some have argued, be detrimental to children's social and emotional skills?

Conclusion

So why are young children so good with technology? It is clear that babies and young children are active explorers and communicators who are motivated to learn and make sense of the world from the relationships, experiences and cultural tools at their disposal. The constant development of digital technologies and an increasing array of user-friendly products have become a familiar part of the world they inhabit.

Children copy the behaviours and actions of the important people in their lives and begin to play with objects and ideas in creative ways as they improve their skills and develop concepts. The immediate responsiveness of many digital products and toys to exploring fingers and visual prompts makes them increasingly accessible and satisfying for even the youngest children. Their often intuitive and playful interactions with an increasingly complex digital culture continue to fascinate and surprise the adults around them.

References

Balbernie, R. (2001). Circuits and circumstances: The neurobiological consequences of early relationship experiences and how they shape later behaviour. *Journal of Child Psychotherapy*, 27(3): 237–255.

Bandura, A. (1997). *Self-Efficacy: The Exercise of Control*. New York: Freeman.

Blair, C. and Diamond, A. (2008). Biological processes in prevention and intervention: The promotion of self-regulation as a means of preventing school failure. *Development and Psychopathology*, 20: 899–911.

Blakemore, S. and Frith, U. (2005). *The Learning Brain: Lessons for Education*. Oxford: Blackwell.

Bransford, J., Brown, A. and Cocking, R. (eds) (2000). *How People Learn: Brain, Mind, Experience and School*. Washington: National Academy Press.

Dowling, M. (2013). *Young Children's Thinking*. London: Sage.

Driscoll, M. P. (2005). *Psychology of Learning for Instruction*. San Francisco: Pearson.

Gerhardt, S. (2004). *Why Love Matters: How Affection Shapes a Baby's Brain*. East Sussex: Brunner-Routledge.

Gibbs, S. (2015). Privacy fears over 'smart' Barbie that can listen to your kids. www.theguardian.com/technology/2015/mar/13/smart-barbie-that-can-listen-to-your-kids-privacy-fears-mattel (accessed April 2015).

Goldberg, S. (2000). *Attachment and Development*. London: Hodder Education.

Gopnik, A. (2009). *The Philosophical Baby*. London: Bodley Head.

Greenhough, W. T., Black, J. E. and Wallace, C. S. (1987). Experience and brain development. *Child Development*, 58(3): 539–559.

Lerner, C. and Barr, R. (2014). *Screen Sense: Setting the Record Straight: Research-Based Guidelines for Screen Use for Children Under 3 Years Old*. Zero to Three. www.zerotothree.org/parenting-resources/screen-sense/screen-sense_wp_final3.pdf (accessed January 2015).

Mareschal, D., Butterworth, B. and Tolmie, A. (2013). *Educational Neuroscience*. Chichester: Wiley-Blackwell.

Marshall, P. J., and Metlzoff, A. N. (2011). Neural mirroring systems: Exploring EEG mu rhythm in human infancy. *Developmental Cognitive Neuroscience*, 1: 110–123.

McPake, J., Plowman, L. and Stephen, C. (2013). Pre-school children creating and communicating with digital technologies in the home. *British Journal of Educational Technology*, 44(3): 421–431.

Murray, L. (2014). *The Psychology of Babies: How Relationships Support Development from Birth to Two*. London: Constable & Robinson.

Ofcom (2014). *Children and Parents: Media Use and Attitudes Report*. http://stakeholders.ofcom.org.uk/binaries/research/media-literacy/media-use-attitudes-14/Childrens_2014_Report.pdf (accessed January 2015).

Palaiologou, I. (2014). Children under five and digital technologies: Implications for early years pedagogy. *European Early Childhood Education Research Journal*, 24(1).

Piaget, J. (1936). *Origins of Intelligence in the Child*. London: Routledge & Kegan Paul.

Plowman, L. and McPake, J. (2013). Seven myths about young children and technology. *Childhood Education*, 89(1): 27–33.

Robbins, J. (2005). Contexts, collaboration, and cultural tools: A sociocultural perspective on researching children's thinking. *Contemporary Issues in Early Childhood*, 6(2): 140–149.

Robson, S. (2010). Self-regulation and metacognition in young children's self-initiated play and reflective dialogue. *International Journal of Early Years Education*, 18(3): 227–241.

Schore, A. N. (2001). Minds in the making: Attachment, the self-organising brain, and developmentally-orientated psychotherapy. *British Journal of Psychotherapy*, 17(3): 299–328.

Seigal, D. J. (1999). *The Developing Mind: Towards a Neurobiology of Interpersonal Experience*. New York: Guilford Press.

Whitebread, D. and Pino-Pasternak, D. (2013). Video analysis of self-regulated learning in social and naturalistic contexts: The case of preschool and primary school children. In S. Volet and M. Vauras (eds), *Interpersonal Regulation of Learning and Motivation Methodological Advances*. Abingdon: Routledge.

Whitebread, D., Coltman, P. and Pino Pasternak, D. (2009). The development of two observational tools for assessing metacognition and self-regulated learning in young children. *Metacognition and Learning*, 4: 63–85.

Wooldridge, M. B. and Shapka, J. (2012). Playing with technology: Mother–toddler interaction scores lower during play with electronic toys. *Journal of Applied Developmental Psychology*, 33: 211–218.

Vygotsky, L. S. (1962). *Thought and Language*. Cambridge, MA: MIT Press.

CHAPTER

3

Language acquisition in a digital age

Louise Dryden

Introduction

As handheld devices, laptops and computers have moved into the everyday lives of most of the population, very young children now have early exposure to a wide variety of different forms of communication in their home environment. This technology enables most children to engage with spoken language(s), as well as with a range of visual texts. These rich digital resources need to be mined by educational settings in order to support children's language and literacy development, and ensure that all children have access to digital as well as paper texts. McLean (2013) suggests that the role of the educator is to encourage children's access to a range of experiences beyond the early years setting, through the medium of technology.

This chapter will explore some of the ways in which young children can experience IT as a means of communication (Marsh and Hallet, 2008), and as a creative tool (Ager, 2003). It will consider ways in which a myriad of sources of information, including talking books, online libraries and digital recording devices can be used to promote verbal discourse (speaking and listening). This chapter will also examine the way in which digital media can be employed to encourage children to interact with on-screen texts, and will address practical ways in which a variety of digital equipment can be used to enhance children's literacy experiences. Technology should be a 'medium of access and construction' (Beauchamp, 2012: 79) and so we also consider multimodal literacies (Flewitt, 2008) and the plethora of material and resources available using quite simple IT devices.

Recent research highlights the need to integrate technological and literacy practices used in the home, into educational settings, but at the same time, one of the stumbling blocks in the way of progress is the lack of confidence expressed by some early years practitioners with regard to their own ability to use IT effectively (Aubrey and Dahl, 2008), and this is explored further in Chapter 6. Resources and techniques which engage children in visual literacies, and materials which can promote early reading and writing practices are examined, in order to encourage students and practitioners to broaden their teaching methods beyond commercially available teaching programs. Another difficulty is the availability of resources, including funding issues which inhibit the use of technology in early years settings. Research by the National Literacy Trust (Formby, 2014) found that 78 per cent of young children had no access to tablet computers.

Spoken communication

The importance of communication skills

The capacity for communication is innate. Babies begin to communicate immediately after birth (Kisilvesky *et al.*, 2009), but Sacks (1989) explains that, unlike other innate skills, human communication cannot be learned in isolation. Children are anxious to communicate, firstly as babies by crying for attention, and later by imitating the human speech they hear around them (Dryden, 2014). However, children need a rich conversational environment in order to learn their first and subsequent languages. Concerns have been raised in recent years that many young children are arriving at early years settings with very poorly developed language skills (ICAN, 2007). This suggests that while children are listening to speech in their home environment, watching television and perhaps engaging with other digital media sources, their own speech does not develop adequately without two-way communication. Therefore, the challenge that is faced by early years educators is to ensure that all children have access to a stimulating and diverse range of verbal expression and that they begin to develop a wide vocabulary.

Traditional early years practice has always emphasised the importance of encouraging children to engage in speaking and listening activities (Brock and Rankin, 2008). Practitioners know that purposeful activities provide open-ended opportunities for young children to communicate with their peers and with adults. For centuries stories and rhymes have captured children's imaginations, enhanced their spoken language and extended their vocabulary. In addition, the benefits of imaginative play, for example, which encourages children to engage in realistic dialogues, was understood by early years pioneers such as Susan Issacs (1885–1948). This has been extended further by recent theories which recognise the supporting role of adults in nurturing children's communication and cognitive skills, in particular through concepts such as sustained shared thinking (Pound, 2009).

The current curriculum documents (DfES, 2012a, 2012b) propose a variety of different ways in which spoken language can be developed through interaction with peers and adults. The Statutory Framework (DfES, 2012a) emphasises the importance of speaking and listening by separating it from literacy, as one of the core areas for development. While the National Literacy Trust (NLT) early years practitioner survey conducted in 2013, found that 80 per cent of the respondents considered the use of technology to be 'supplemental rather than central' to the learning environment (Formby, 2014), let us consider ways in which technology can enhance the development of children's spoken communication.

Benefits of technology to language acquisition

There is a plethora of equipment which can be used to provide opportunities for children to listen and respond to the spoken word in dynamic ways (see Table 3.1

below). However, as stated above, it is important for technology to be used as a tool for two-way communication; passive listening is not as powerful as experiences where children are encouraged to be active participants.

Speaking

Technology provides numerous opportunities for children to communicate their ideas and feelings: repeating vocabulary, stories, songs and rhymes using adult-modelled language, etc. In addition, it enables them to produce unique speech, providing a platform for them to discuss, narrate, recount, explain, problem-solve and negotiate verbally with others (see Table 3.1 below). Using walkie-talkies, for example, encourages them to communicate with someone they cannot see, which is a skill many young children find challenging. Microphones and recording equipment also enable them to practise giving instructions (Addison, 2012), expressing their ideas and feelings, and giving them the opportunity to listen back and critique their own language. Recording also allows them to erase and re-record if they feel dissatisfied with their first attempt. Kennington and Meaton (2009) suggest the use of very simple equipment such as 'Talking Tins'. Some children will be familiar with podcasts and Skype at home, and these too can be incorporated into the early years curriculum. Young children also thoroughly enjoy the opportunity to use karaoke to join in with familiar songs and nursery rhymes.

Using the Interactive Whiteboard (IWB) can encourage small groups of children to engage in learning with or without an adult. The large screen makes the IWB a social learning tool and is a very effective teaching tool at circle times (Kennington and Meaton, 2009). The IWB facilitates discussion on topics not available in the setting, making it possible to display pictures to stimulate discussion (Jesson and Peacock, 2012), including the use of children's photographs or video of themselves and familiar objects and places. Using the board itself encourages the use of a range of communicative language skills and vocabulary, stimulating debate and verbal negotiation among the children, using a range of personalised resources, for example children could take photographs of an activity such as cooking and use the board to put them in sequence. By working alongside the children on the IWB, the practitioner is able to support and encourage children's learning and development. The IWB also provides opportunities to involve parents and carers by putting together a slideshow of the activities undertaken in a session, which can then be shared and discussed.

Role-play areas

Technology also has a place in imaginative play areas, where for example, Price (2009) suggests videos can be played as a backdrop, providing scenery and stimulating the children's play by setting the scene/action. Alternatively, the children can be encouraged to engage in role play using a sequence of photos on the IWB (Addison, 2012). Children can also gain familiarity with technology by using digital equipment as part of their role play. They can handle tools that they see in the world about them, experiment and take control, learning about these objects and their place in the world, supporting and extending technological language in their explanations and discussion.

Technology can encourage children who may be reluctant to speak to use their voices in playful ways. James and Cane (2009) describe a child who was embarrassed by their accent and was reluctant to speak, but who became confident after enjoying using a voice changer.

Listening

For many years children have had the opportunity to listen to taped stories, where an adult reads aloud from a story book. This is in itself a valuable experience, but newer technology allows us to extend this. For example, children can record themselves retelling a familiar story using a digital recorder, and then share with their peers. They can also listen to a story told by one of their peers, or hear an adult telling a story they narrated with help from the children. Children enjoy hearing the same

TABLE 3.1 Speaking and listening

Equipment	How it can be used	Benefits	EAL
Taped stories Headphones	Listen, or follow story in a book	Opportunity to listen in a quiet, intimate way	Dual language books
Digital recorders Microphones Talking photo albums/ cards/Talking Tins	Adult tells a story Children tell stories, recount visit or outing Follow oral instructions	As above, but more personalised Careful listening without visual clues	Bilingual adult records a story in their community language. (see case study 1 below)
Walkie-talkies, two-way radios, mobile phones	Talk at a distance Give instructions	Practise making themselves understood when not face to face	Use first language
Recordable binoculars	Record speech while exploring	Using descriptive language	Record short bursts of speech in any language
Talking clipboard	Record voice whilst mark-making Listen to instructions left by adult	Combine mark-making and communication	Use language for a purpose
IWB	Using images for discussion (fiction and non-fiction), which provide opportunities to recount and engage in verbal interactions	Bring topics into the setting which would only otherwise be accessible in book form	Provide clear illustrations which children can recognise
Videos	Follow a storyline Listen to dialogue Discuss plot	Discuss; anticipate the action	Support understanding through visual clues
Slideshows visualiser	Provide a series of images	Children can discuss/ narrate	Can discuss in own language
PC/tablets Games	Listen to stories, follow instructions	Learning supported by visual clues	In first language/or supports English

story repeated many times, and so headphones and digital materials model the use of expression in reading and enable children to make the connections between text on a page and text as it sounds, which is critically important in literacy development (DCSF, 2008). Young children need to be able to play with and explore technology, which can provide a sense of empowerment (Price, 2009). Equipment such as multi-link headphones enables them to work together (Kennington and Meaton, 2009).

Case study 1

Bilal and Shazia are new to English. A bilingual worker in their nursery is able to record a version of an unfamiliar picture book in Urdu. They are introduced to the book in Urdu first and enjoy the richness of the descriptive language. They listen several times using headphones and like sitting together to share the experience. When the picture book is read in English a few days later, they are better able to follow the storyline and participate enthusiastically with the other children. Later in the week, they are encouraged to retell the story together using a digital recorder.

Special Educational Needs and Disabilities (SEND)

Digital technology can meet all children's needs and provide access to effective tools to support their literacy learning and development. Voice recording enables those with visual impairments to enjoy stories and story-telling. They can record their own voices and listen to stories and instructions recorded by others. Most new PCs support voice recognition, and programs such as Siri are available for tablets. For children with hearing impairments there are newly developed avatars which act as digital signers.

Accessing/reading texts

Developing the capacity to read is fundamental to educational achievement, and it has long been recognised that young children should be exposed to a wide variety of texts long before they are capable of reading for themselves (Browne, 2009; Meek, 1991). Publishing houses have responded to the market and many exciting, vibrant children's books are made available every day. Picture books enable young children to retell familiar stories, using the illustrations as clues. Children also enjoy browsing through unfamiliar picture books and texts, extracting meaning from the illustrations; good children's literature has many layers, with stories and subtexts that are gradually revealed (Meek, 1991). Above all, reading is an active search for meaning (Marsh and Hallet, 2008). See Table 3.3 for uses of technology for accessing and reading texts.

McLean (2013) argues that this need for a rich literary environment should include the use of technology. McLean (2013) suggests that the way literacy is conceived has changed over the past twenty years with the advent of new technological advances, and that a mutually beneficial relationship has developed which is shaping our sociocultural literacy. For example, the proliferation of applications for smartphones and tablet computers in recent years has enabled children to access traditional storybooks as interactive experiences (Roskos *et al.*, 2014). Moody *et al.*'s (2010) study found that pre-school children demonstrated higher levels of persistence when listening to stories presented in an e-book format, led by an adult. However, the children appeared to be more responsive verbally during traditional storybook telling, than when sharing e-books with an adult reader.

In 2013 the National Literacy Trust (NLT) conducted an online survey with 362 invited practitioners who work with three- to five-year-olds in order to explore how they support children's language and communication skills. One of the main aims was to explore how often practitioners and children engaged in reading-related activities when in settings, and how often they use technology, in particular touchscreen devices, in their setting. Of those with access to a tablet computer, children were more likely to use the device at least once in a typical week with an adult as opposed to print books, which children were more likely to browse by themselves (Formby, 2014). In the study, practitioners were more likely to say children enjoyed looking at books a lot with an adult rather than without an adult (95.9 per cent versus 66.9 per cent). However, practitioners stated that children enjoyed using a tablet computer irrespective of whether they used the device with or without an adult (76.1 per cent versus 73.7 per cent). Furthermore, practitioners were more likely to say children enjoy using a tablet computer a lot without an adult than they were to say children enjoy looking at or reading books a lot without an adult (73.7 per cent versus 66.9 per cent) (Formby, 2014). Table 3.2 indicates why practitioners think children enjoy using tablet computers.

TABLE 3.2 Why do practitioners think children enjoy using tablet computers?

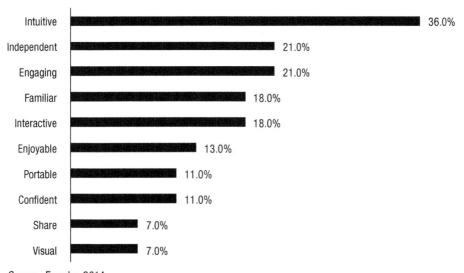

Source: Formby, 2014.

Over one-third (36.0 per cent) of practitioners say that children enjoy using tablet computers because they are intuitive to use. One-fifth of practitioners (21.0 per cent) mentioned children can use tablet computers independently and one-fifth (21.0 per cent) mentioned they are engaging. Nearly one-fifth of practitioners say children enjoy using tablet computers because they are interactive (18.0 per cent).

Benefits of digital technology to reading development

Reading screens

Currently, children are able to browse and surf on TVs, PCs and tablets; even toddlers are fascinated by the opportunities afforded by touchscreen technologies. Children soon recognise the symbols (see Chapter 4) which lead to their favourite pages/characters, and in this way children can work beyond their conventional reading age, as there is seldom the need to rely on text since icons and images convey information (Beauchamp, 2012). Many children will have experience using console games in the home environment and are adept at navigating their way around quite complex screens, even though they are not yet 'readers'. In this way, computers are challenging our ideas with regard to what it means to be literate.

Visual literacies

Modes of communication have been expanding rapidly in recent years, and the printed word is only one way in which we take meaning from texts. Writers such as Kress (1997) have explored the idea that reading is multimodal, that is, text can be 'read' in many different ways. Kress goes so far as to suggest that we are entering a 'new age of hieroglyphics' (1997: xvii). We are constantly surrounded by visual stimuli, in the street as well as in the home, and from an early age children are familiar with videos, films, and radios as well as computers (QCA/UKLA 2004).

Video games and screen technology are perfect media for exploring visually exciting texts. Use of still and moving images and sound are ideal for young children to begin to develop visual literacies and links can be made with home experiences (Din, 2009). Furthermore, screen texts are very flexible and are often non-linear. Very young children soon learn to navigate around websites (such as CBeebies), or use apps in a non-linear fashion, making choices unavailable in printed books. Even traditional printed material can be enlivened using fonts and symbols to provide additional meaning. The development of visual literacies enables a reader or a writer to access or express themselves through drawings, diagrams and other symbolic systems.

Narrative

An important aspect of learning to be literate is to develop an understanding of how texts work (Meek, 1991). Alongside print books, there is a variety of digital texts where stories suitable for young children are available to download. Many publishers have recognised the potential of digital media to enhance children's enjoyment of texts (e.g. Ladybird). Many popular children's books are now available in a digital format and picture books are particularly effective when viewed on a large screen. 'Talking books' give children the opportunity to see the written text as it is being read aloud. This encourages the child to see how the spoken word is matched to the corresponding written symbols, particularly when the words are highlighted as they are read aloud. In addition, the child is made aware of the direction of print, read from left to right in English. CBeebies and the British Council websites, for example, have numerous short videos which include traditional stories, with graphics and musical accompaniment. It is possible to download some well-known, contemporary texts, and some are available for free on YouTube.

Apart from written texts, children are exposed to a variety of different media, including digital forms such as television programmes, films and DVDs. These all contribute to children's understanding of narrative, and the exploration of media texts helps them to develop a broader understanding of how texts work (Marsh and Hallet, 2008). This can be translated in their own story-narratives. Marsh (in Marsh and Hallet, 2008) describes how young children were encouraged to make animated films using Playmobil figures, filming with a small camera. This type of activity helps children to understand compositional processes such as sequencing, which can later be translated into writing their own narratives. The British Film Institute (BFI) was involved in a project in 2003 which produced a series of short animated films to be used in the Foundation Stage. These films gave the children opportunities to begin to recognise the elements that are used to build up a film, as well as understand story conventions. Children also have the opportunity to create an avatar/superhero (Addison, 2012) using software such as can be seen on the Club Penguin website.

Screen exercises

Many software companies have seen the potential in producing programs which help children to practise literacy skills. This has been done with varying degrees of success; the best programs being designed by those companies that include teachers on their design teams. Exercises which teach sequencing, cloze procedure and in particular phonics (skills advocated by educators including Browne, 2009) have proved popular with children who enjoy the competitive aspects of these programs. These are valuable but need to come with a health warning. Sometimes they are too simple and do not challenge the children enough, or alternatively progress can be too swift and the child is frustrated by the complexity of the game. Using large screens on which to play word games promotes discussion among the players and observers (Goouch and Lambirth, 2011).

Special Educational Needs and Disabilities (SEND)

Screen texts are extremely useful when working with children with visual impairments. Illustrations and fonts can be enlarged to ensure that all children can see shared texts on tablets and on an IWB. Also, the colour of fonts and backgrounds can be adjusted to meet particular needs, such as dyslexia. There is also a range of input devices for children with physical disabilities, such as switches, joysticks and eye gaze technology (see www.inclusive.co.uk).

TABLE 3.3 Accessing and reading texts

Equipment	How can they be used	Benefits	EAL
Taped stories Headphones	Follow the story by looking at the book while listening to the words	Opportunity to understand how texts work. Page turning and anticipation of storyline	Dual language books
IWB Slideshows	Accessing a wide variety of visual and written texts, perhaps with simple captions. Use different effects to order and reveal information systematically	Introduce large print and different fonts which children can begin to 'read' together	Children can recognise illustrations which explain new vocabulary
Visualiser	Project any text onto a large screen	Share any text with a group of children	Commentary/story can be told in any language
PC/tablets Games	Opening programs, navigating around screens and 'reading' instructions	Learning supported by visual clues	In first language, or supports English
Photocopier	Duplicate and/or enlarge texts	Support reading opportunities	Gather examples of different scripts/alphabets

Promoting literacy experiences

For centuries literacy was the only method by which people could communicate at a distance, giving speech a lasting quality. We can access authors from past centuries, providing us with valuable insights into their thoughts, attitudes and an understanding of the societies in which they lived. With the invention of symbolic representations found in cultures BCE, humans began to record information in a variety of ways. There is a distinction to be drawn between *writing systems* which transcribe the spoken word and *symbolic systems* which can be understood visually by people who speak a variety of languages, or none at all. While early manuscripts were handwritten by scribes, the advent of the printing press provided a simpler way to make duplicate texts. More recently, innovations in technology enabled people to send written communication first by telegraph, and now via the internet.

Children first begin to make marks at a very early stage in their development; babies in their highchairs enjoy moving their fingers through spilt food (Dryden, 2005). This interest in mark-marking continues in an ad-hoc manner for the first couple of years of life during which they become more skilful at manipulating and controlling a variety of different tools. At first there is no intention to communicate ideas; it is the pure joy of movement, colour and shape. Many adults who are new to working with children make the error of asking what their picture is about – this is often met with a blank stare. However, over time children begin to draw and attempt to reproduce symbols they see in their environment (Dryden, 2004), including written alphabets in their home languages. This mark-making develops into an intention to make meaning from the symbols and letters, known as emergent writing (Riley, 2006).

Benefits of technology to mark-making development

Today, mark-making can be extended to include a variety of skills relating to technology. Extremely young children are fascinated by screens and, given the opportunity, enjoy manipulating items on a touchscreen tablet or PC. Most computers have a paint/draw program which allows a child to use a mouse or their finger to experiment, using a variety of tools, colours and techniques. These can be printed out to produce a permanent record of their work. See Table 3.4 for examples of the use of technology for mark-making.

Interactive Whiteboards (IWB)

IWBs are an excellent way of modelling writing behaviours for young children in group settings (see Figure 3.1). Adults can be seen using the board to draw, make notes and move information around the screen. The screens are often sited quite high above ground level and for this reason it is important for a platform to be erected beneath the screen for the children to stand on safely or, ideally, made available at child height. This allows them free access to the screen without adult supervision and the dimensions of an IWB offer children opportunity to use large arm movements (Lowe, 2009).

FIGURE 3.1 A child using a program on an IWB during free play.

It can take time for staff and children to learn how to use the commercially produced 'electronic pens', but a large soft paintbrush is an ideal alternative. These provide suitable pressure and are much easier for small hands to manipulate. They also enable children to reach higher up the screen where the controls are often sited.

PCs and tablets

The possibilities for children to produce attractive texts are exciting and limitless on the computer. Early software often promoted pedestrian phonic and word-matching games, but current programs such as 2Simple and Clicker 6 now offer excellent software appropriate for even the youngest of children. These products support children's earliest attempts at writing and enable the child to make and send e-cards (Price, 2009), make lists, design badges and labels, and build simple texts with captions, which can also include animations. Children can also be encouraged to design a set of instructions for Bee-Bot® (Addison, 2012) for example (see the case study below).

Case study 2

Rob, a reception class teacher in a primary school, has been given a programmable toy for his class to use. He begins by introducing it to the whole class during a carpet session and the children are very excited by it. He demonstrates how the controls work, picks a couple of children to try it out and says that they will all get an opportunity to use it working in small groups. He has cards with directional words printed on them. He encourages the children to recognise these as 'sight words', and they practise raising right and left limbs etc. Later in the day Rob puts the toy in a quiet corner of the room and sets the cards beside them for the children to use (see Figure 3.2).

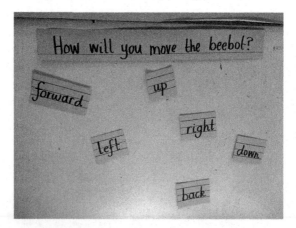

FIGURE 3.2 Composing instructions for the Bee-Bot®.

In subsequent weeks, he will introduce a series of mats which provide scenarios for the children to navigate around, and he will introduce increasingly complex written instructions for the children to follow. As an extension, he later puts wipeboards in the area for the children to write their own instructions.

There is convincing evidence that play situations are excellent for promoting emergent literacy (Hall and Robinson, 2003; DCSF, 2008). Defunct equipment such as old telephones, PCs and laptops give children an opportunity to act out literate behaviours. Taking this idea further, a tablet can be used to take food orders in the play café, print out prescriptions in the 'hospital' or catalogue equipment in the 'garage'.

There are two elements to writing texts, using compositional and transcriptional skills. Voice recognition enables children to compose orally and have their ideas transposed into print. This is particularly helpful for children when they are at the early stages of becoming a writer. It removes the need to concentrate on handwriting and spelling, and allows them to concentrate on the content of their compositions.

Keyboards

Young children can soon find their way around the QWERTY keyboard, and seem to adapt quickly to the distinction between lower- and upper-case letters, and cope extremely well with adult-sized keyboards. However, some manufacturers produce larger versions with bigger keys (particularly useful with children with disabilities) and there are also some keyboards with lower-case letters. A smaller mouse may be better for little hands to grasp and manipulate.

Case study 3

Several years ago I carried out some research on children's use of keyboards. I coined the term 'emergent typing' (Dryden, 2007) where young children play on a keyboard and produce strings of letters and symbols which mimic written text but are unreadable; this mirrors children's early attempts at handwritten scripts which look like text but are nonsense strings of letters. The children in this project were reception-aged and I worked with a small group using Kowari, an early program which set up a secure, child-friendly e-mail system.

The program provided each child with a character from a fairy tale (Goldilocks) and they 'wrote' and sent postcards to other characters from the story. This was a simple but effective idea, because young children would struggle to compose messages without a context. The children were thrilled to see their drawings and 'captions' sent from one PC to another in the form of postcards. At first the children tapped indiscriminately at the keys. However, the children were encouraged to seek out and type the letters of their names, and over the research period some children began to type captions using words from a list related to the Goldilocks story.

There is a debate concerning whether children should be taught to touch-type in primary school. Certainly adults (including this author) would be more efficient if we could type accurately at speed, but many people can reach impressive typing speeds using just two or four fingers. In addition, touchscreen technology and smaller digital equipment such as mobile phones have necessitated the development of new skills where typing is carried out using only the tip of a finger or writing with a stylus on a touchscreen. It remains to be seen what effects touchscreens and other digital media have on children's emergent writing. Indeed this debate can be explored further – some might argue that in years to come attitudes towards the written word (and spelling) will change, and that people may turn away from handwriting as a form of communication. We may soon be using speech to text far more.

Special Educational Needs and Disabilities (SEND)

Large keyboards can support children with disabilities and assist the dexterity of those with poor manipulative skills. The size of both screens and keyboards can be advantageous to those with visual impairments. Voice-to-text software also enables children with various conditions to see their words transformed into written text.

TABLE 3.4 Mark-making

Equipment	How can they be used	Benefits	EAL
IWB	Mark-making on a large scale 'Drag and drop' words to form a caption	Satisfaction of producing an image or caption	
Keyboards	Recognise letters and other symbols	Distinguish between lower- and upper-case letters	
PC/tablets	Use screens to make marks, draw or type text	Produce satisfying products which can be printed off	Can use different alphabets
Bee-Bots®	Write instructions	Writing for a purpose	Learn directional language
Video and camera stimuli	Compose a caption to go with the pictures	Writing for a purpose	Biliterate opportunities
E-mails	Send simple texts	Communicate and express themselves in print	
Printer	To make hard copies of children's drawing and mark-making	Produce a permanent record of a piece of work	Can include text in more than one language
Word-processing software (e.g. 2Write, Clicker 6)	To compose simple text	Provides a structure for child-initiated composition	Text can be entered in a variety of languages

Practical applications

While preparing to write this chapter, I interviewed a group of early years practitioners in a local primary school and carried out an observation in a reception classroom. The teachers were very enthusiastic about the use of technology in their classes and said that the children had opportunities to use a range of software and equipment. The nursery staff said that they had cameras, and Bee-Bots®, iPads and PCs, microphones and voice recorders, as well as video equipment and IWBs. They said there were a range of games that they accessed via the internet which the children enjoyed using on the IWB, and that they also used software on the PC, though this was limited to some extent by their purchasing power. They said that their advice was often sought by parents on apps and games for children to use at home, and they had been very fortunate when one parent gave them access to a set of published phonic programs.

A cautionary note was that many resources on the internet were from the USA, and therefore pronunciation sometimes proved problematic, particularly with phonic exercises, rhymes etc. They also reported that while the iPads were very popular with the children, they always used the touchscreen facility and never the keyboards (see Chapter 1).

All these activities were very popular with the children, with queues forming around equipment, so they had instituted various strategies for ensuring that all children had time (such as using timers to avoid some children from monopolising the resources). However, they felt that the children were generally patient about turn-taking, and that it was an opportunity for the children to work collaboratively. Onlookers were also engaged, developing communication skills as they discussed the action, and gave advice or prompted the child who was using the program.

In the reception class the children used more sophisticated programs and were able to self-regulate more effectively. On the afternoon I observed, the children were choosing from a wide range of activities around the room, including several employing technology. This class were able to use the IWB with confidence and without adult supervision, only requesting help from the class teacher when they wanted to switch programs. The way the class was organised demonstrated that these resources could be integrated very naturally into the reception class curriculum.

DISCUSSION TOPICS

- What are the benefits or disadvantages of children being exposed to technology in terms of language acquisition?
- Is it necessary for children to practise neat handwriting?
- What effects have/will touchscreen and other digital media have on children's emergent writing?
- Will the written word (and spelling in particular) change as people turn to digital forms of communication?

Conclusion

While literacy practices in many homes provide a rich introduction to young children's understanding of what it means to be literate, many early years settings appear somewhat reluctant to fully embrace technology as a vibrant addition to the literary-learning environment (Aubrey and Dahl, 2008). This is despite the clear messages embedded in key curriculum documentation and training materials (such as Letters and Sounds, DfES, 2007). Some textbooks on early literacy development still fail to adequately address the benefits of capturing children's interest in the written word using widely available technological resources. This suggests that there still remains some concern among traditionalists who consider that young children's literacy development should be unencumbered by modern practices. However, it is also clear that children need to be digitally literate in today's society.

References

Addison, I. (2012). *ICT Essentials*. London: Rising Stars Ltd.

Ager, R. (2003). *Information and Communications Technology in Primary Schools: Children or Computers in Control?* London: Fulton.

Aubrey, C. and Dahl, S. (2008). *A Review of the Evidence on the Use of ICT in the Early Years Foundation Stage*. London: BECTA.

Beauchamp, G. (2012). *ICT in the Primary School: From Pedagogy to Practice*. London: Routledge.

Brock, A. and Rankin, C. (2008). *Communication, Language and Literacy from Birth to Five*. London: Sage.

Browne, A. (2009). *Developing Language and Literacy 3–8*. London: Sage.

DCSF (2008). *Mark Making Matters*. Nottingham: DCSF Publications.

DfE (2012a). *Statutory Framework for the Early Years Foundation Stage*. Nottingham: DfE Publications.

DfE (2012b). *Developmental Matters in Early Years Foundation Stage*. London: DfE.

DfES (2007). *Letters and Sounds: Principles and Practice of High Quality Phonics*. Nottingham: DfES Publications.

Din, R. (2009). Visual literacy – Bollywood style. *English 4–11*, 37: 20–21.

Dryden, L. (2004). Showing signs. *Nursery World*, 22 April, pp. 22–23.

Dryden, L. (2005). Language and literacy. In L. Dryden, P. Mukherji, R. Forbes, and L. Pound, *Essential Early Years*. London: Hodder Arnold.

Dryden, L. (2007). Emergent typing. *English 4–11*, 31: 15–18.

Dryden, L. (2014). Communication, literacy and ICT. In P. Mukherji and L. Dryden. *Foundations of Early Childhood: Principles and Practice*. London: Sage.

Flewitt, R. (2008). Multimodal literacies. In J. Marsh and E. Hallet (eds), *Desirable Literacies. Approaches to Language and Literacy in the Early Years* (2nd edn). London: Sage.

Formby, S. (2014). *Practitioner Perspectives: Children's Use of Technology in the Early Years*. Harlow: National Literacy Trust/Pearson.

Goouch, K. and Lambirth, A. (2011). *Teaching Early Reading and Phonics: Creative Approaches to Early Literacy*. London: Sage.

Hall, N. and Robinson, A. (2003). *Exploring Writing and Play in the Early Years*. London: David Fulton.

ICAN (2007). Language and social exclusion. I CAN Talk Series, Issue 4. www.ICAN.org.uk (accessed September 2012).

James, K. and Cane, C. (2009). Giving children a voice by using ICT. In H. Price (2009). *The Really Useful Book of ICT in the Early Years*. London: Routledge.

Jesson, J. and Peacock, G. (2012). *The Really Useful ICT Book*. Oxon: Routledge.

Kennington, L. and Meaton, J. (2009). ICT and the Early Years curriculum. In H. Price, *The Really Useful Book of ICT in the Early Years*. London: Routledge.

Kisilvesky, B. S., Hains, S. M. J., Brown, C. A., Lee, C. T. and Cowperthwaite, B. (2009). Fetal sensitivity to properties of maternal speech and language. *Infant Behaviour Development*, 32(1): 59–71.

Kress, G. (1997). *Before Writing: Rethinking the Paths of Literacy*. London: Routledge.

Lowe, H. (2009). Children's independence and ICT. In H. Price, *The Really Useful Book of ICT in the Early Years*. London: Routledge.

Marsh, J. and Hallet, E. (eds) (2008). *Desirable Literacies. Approaches to Language and Literacy in the Early Years* (2nd edn). London: Sage.

McLean, K. (2013). Literacy and technology in the early years of education: Looking to the familiar to inform educator practice. *Australasian Journal of Early Childhood*, 38(4): 30–41.

Meek, M. (1991). *On Being Literate*. London: Bodley Head.

Moody, A. K., Justice, L. M. and Cabell, S. Q. (2010). Electronic verus traditional storybooks: Relative influence on pre-school children's engagement and communication. *Journal of Early Childhood Literacy*, 10(3): 294–313.

Pound, L. (2009). *How Children Learn: 3. Contemporary Thinking and Theorists*. London: MA Education.

Price, H. (2009). *The Really Useful Book of ICT in the Early Years*. London: Routledge.

QCA/UKLA (2004). *More Than Words. Multimodal Texts in the Classroom*. London: QCA.

Riley, J. (2006). *Language and Literacy 3–7*. London: Sage.

Roskos, K., Burstein, K., Shang, Y. and Gray, E. (2014). Young children's engagement with e-books at school. Does device matter? *Journal of Early Childhood Literacy*, 4(1).

Sacks, O. (1989). *Seeing Voices*. Los Angeles, California: Stoddart.

Useful websites

www.bbc.co.uk/cbeebies
www.literacytrust.org.uk
www.ukla.org
http://homerton.cambs.sch.uk/information-for-practioners/ict-in-the-early-years/

The power of digital symbolic representation

Jacqueline Harding

FIGURE 4.1 Symbols are meaningful.

Swiping images is natural to them ... they understand all about tapping screens to make things happen as well as the action of swiping to move things on.
(Mum of eighteen-month-old and three-year-old,
Tomorrow's Child research, 2014)

FIGURE 4.2 Images guide the navigation of content.

Multimodal representation systems permeate a young child's contemporary world and the environment that has been created appears to be as natural to them as the provision of books, comics, paper and crayons were to children only a few generations ago. When asked to define digital symbolic representation or to explain its function, its paradoxical nature becomes apparent. Furthermore, questions concerning its value, use and place within the young child's life has been constantly raised and few scholars are in agreement. This chapter explores the landscape of digital symbolic representation, the views of parents and practitioners as to its function, and how it might usefully be employed in a young child's life within an emerging new play paradigm.

Results of a small-scale online study carried out in 2014 by Tomorrow's Child among 58 adults with diverse responsibilities for children, ranging from parents, grandparents, carers, and educators to students of one- to seven-year-olds, will usefully contribute to the discussion. The work of Marsh (2005, 2010a, 2010b), Buckingham (1996) and Kress (2003) in particular will be drawn upon as voices of sanity within a digitally suspicious world that fears the erosion of the written word.

Make way for new communication forms

The screen is now the dominant site of texts; it is the site which shapes the imagination of the current generation around communication … This does not mean that writing cannot appear on screen, but when it does, it will be appearing there subordinated to the logic of the visual.

(Kress, 2003: 166)

Over the past four decades, technological developments have led to significant changes in the ways in which we communicate through both spoken language and written text. The layout and presentation of text have moved to a new level of importance and digital technology is reconfiguring the relationship between images and words (symbolic representation).

Importantly, it appears that young children perceive the relationship between image and text quite differently to adults. The value that these digital natives place on images is, I suggest, higher than those of us who are digital immigrants. It is becoming increasingly important that as practitioners, parents and all who are concerned for the education of the young child that we should begin to see the world through the child's eyes.

One of the most significant results of the abovementioned small-scale study was that it revealed the relative position of symbols to texts such as storybooks: 90 per cent of those surveyed in the two to five year age range, regarded the 'reading of images/symbols/pictures/photographs/videos to be as important as reading traditional texts for children'. It was also noteworthy that 87 per cent believed that young children are active participants in their media use. Of course, a more comprehensive study needs to be conducted to confirm these findings but, nevertheless, the results correlate well with other studies (Marsh *et al.*, 2005).

The power of digital media to engage and involve the child was consistently agreed across the age ranges surveyed, with over 90 per cent in the one to two year age range, stating that they would rate their child's level of engagement and involvement as point 4 on a 0–5 scale, with 5 being the highest level. Similarly, in the Digital Beginnings study, parents were positive about the role of new media in the lives of their young children (Marsh *et al.*, 2005).

When can a child be called literate?

The definition of literacy is expanding. This reconfiguration is taking place as fast as hardware becomes outmoded and replaced – offering more and more sophisticated ways to represent 'text'. The word 'literacy' traditionally refers to the ability to read and write print-based media sources, such as in the form of books. Researchers (Buckingham, 2003) propose that the use of all forms of media must be included in the repertoire of literacy skills in order to be considered literate. Other scholars (Bazalgette, 1991) emphasise the need for children to be involved in critical analysis and practical work in their media education, which necessarily includes multimodal literacies: screen-based and all digital texts.

There is no doubt that these multimodal texts are demanding a rethink of what it means to be literate; historical definitions of literacy are now insufficient. These texts are changing reader expectations, and the ways they go about constructing meaning: multimodal texts dictate to the reader new ways of guiding the eye across the page or screen while simultaneously presenting them with sound, speech, intonation, gesture and movement. My research over the last ten years has concerned itself with this conceptual conundrum. Gradually, it dawned on me that children are encountering texts through a completely different set of lenses with new assumptions about the organization of the text – including how they deal with voices, still images and video motion as well as written text. New literacies, which encompass words and symbols, confront the 'reader' with the need to analyse multiple representations. This new language is multimodal and multilayered. The demands it places on the child are complex: the need to construct meaning from images and employ critical thinking in order to make sense of it all and fully integrate the meanings so that a holistic point of comprehension can be achieved.

Media literacy, in a broader sense, has been investigated for over twenty years and Buckingham (2003) provides a suitable definition while acknowledging that confusion remains as to its function: 'something we use when we want to communicate with people indirectly' (Buckingham, 2003: 5). He further proposes that the different forms of media are 'representations of the world' (2003: 3). So, for Buckingham, media literacy concerns the combinations of written and spoken language, sounds, images and symbols used by these forms of communication (Buckingham, 2003).

Moreover, Kress (2003) discusses the affordances of mode and facilities of media as a move away from text dominance to the medium of the screen with its use of image. The belief that digital technology is reconfiguring the relationship between images and words at great speed is resulting in the expansion of our existing definition of literacy. As fast as the hardware for digital technology becomes outmoded and replaced it offers more and more sophisticated ways to represent 'text'. It demands the inclusion of a wide variety of media, including computers, video games, television and the internet. Written text dictates the compulsory flow and reading path whereas 'the reading path of the image is of a more open nature with several entry points' (Kress, 2003: 3). The move away from *telling the world* to *showing the world* (Kress 2003: 140) as typified by Facebook and selfies depicts the profound shift in the act of 'reading'. Kress (2003: 140) also discusses how, in a Western text-driven society, there is a move to 'the appearance of an image without accommodating text': thus, most importantly, allowing the image to stand in its own right. Several researchers (Kress, 2003; McGonigal, 2012) also provide evidence of how in the use of online games, children employ skills of visual analysis, manual dexterity, and strategic and tactical decision-making at meta-levels. It must be acknowledged that children, while reading the text (which remains on screen fleetingly), are simultaneously listening to the musical score and dialogue from characters. There is no doubt that children have little difficulty deciphering visually saturated screens while adults typically cannot 'read' at that pace. The debate concerning whether text-based reading really is in decline must be subject to the fact that there are greater demands for faster reading patterns, which also include images and sounds to which the child must attend. Perhaps, as Kress proposes, this does not indicate a decline in standards of reading at all. Traditional means of accessing and making sense of text occur over a limited, concentrated period for a specific purpose and Kress (2003) proposes that children are now reading for information that relates to *the moment*. Donaldson, in *Children's Minds*, discusses Piaget's proposal for how a child experiences life – 'he lives in the state of the moment, not bothering himself with how things were previously, with the relation of one state to those which come before or after it. His world is like a film run slowly' (1986: 20).

Frederick R. Barnard, in the early part of the twentieth century, famously said, 'A picture is worth a thousand words'. Perhaps at some point in our lives, we all sense that an image or a picture says something that we are unable to express? It feels … just beyond words.

Semiotics and new ways of communicating and socialising

The field of semiotics is helpful to this discussion. Movement, gesture, music, sounds and images are the modes that children begin to recognise, understand and manipulate in order to be become literate. It appears that even young children are actively poised to negotiate the territory in order to meet their varied cultural and social needs (Marsh et al., 2005). Marsh asserts that:

> Children engage in a semiotic world in which texts in different modes are conceptually linked. They do not see a neat dichotomy between print and televisual texts as they move seamlessly from one mode to another in their quest for meaning-making ... they use visual, literate, oral and corporeal modes of communication in a range of multi-modal practices.
>
> (Marsh 2003: 43)

From a purely practical standpoint, semiotics plays a major role when attempting to understand the lens through which children construct meaning from these multimodal texts. Employing semiotic analysis enables researchers to delve below the surface of the signs. Semioticians discuss users of texts as readers, generally preferring the term 'reader' to 'receiver'. This implies an *active* process of decoding. Saussure (1986 [1916]) addressed this concept by discussing how the linguistic sign does not unite a thing and a name, but a concept and a sound image. Semiotics is about meaning-making and was pivotal to my search for the meaning and nature of media play. Of course, the action of humans is to make meaning and Kress (2003) asserts that meaning-makers make changes in their learning, to their resources and to themselves. However, as Parker proposes (2006: 158), perhaps there is a need to go beyond semiotics and establish new accounts of pedagogy.

Active participants

I make it happen.

> (Child aged three using new software on a laptop)

So, is semiosis separate from learning? No. It's about asking the same question only through a different lens: a multimodal approach to learning. That which I engage in is remaking the environment and we recognise now that learning comes through different modes. In fact, questions need to be asked such as 'When are we not learning?', 'When does learning not occur?' Further, if we know that young children are meaning-makers surely we need to assess them differently and attend to their process of learning – for example, which of their senses were they utilising? Young children, I propose, unmistakeably excel in the use of their full range of senses and this affords them ease of access to a multimodal approach to learning. Indeed, Marsh and Hallet (2010) assert that children will move fluidly between communication systems, choosing to switch between modalities as the need arises. Marsh's work in exploring young children's literacy practices through Club Penguin (Marsh 2010b) investigates the way in which children participate in exchanges with others. The precise patterns of meaning-making in digital texts is only just emerging.

FIGURE 4.3 A push of a button is all it takes.

Children have learned early on in their digital experiences that text may offer more than one entry point, whereas in traditional text there may have been only one – the top left-hand side of the page. A website, for example, is likely to have three to six entry points, even for those productions that are dedicated to the under-sevens (e.g. CBeebies online). Are the multiplicity of entry points a positive aspect? I propose that indeed this adds value to the learning experience as it offers children multiple ways of accessing the material they desire from a number of starting points. 'The new technology has changed unidirectionality into bidirectionality' (Kress 2003: 6).

Digital image-based play

If it is now widely believed that play for a young child is their work, and it can be seen that children are 'working' very hard at this new kind of digital play. Of course, the influence of this new kind of digital play with a variety of symbols is hitherto unexplored. Carol Fox (1993) discusses her desire for an alternative word for play – one indicating something of the intensity and effort that co-exists with its inconsequential, ephemeral natural. Through my own research, I have begun to propose a new form of play: 'immersive digital play' (IDP) built upon digital symbolic representation as I, too, sought a new description for this form of play. However, just how play functions and the intricacies of its nature (most critically within a media-saturated environment) are not well discussed or documented, let alone agreed. Indeed, in Bruner *et al.*'s *Play – It's Role Development and Evolution* (1976: 70), the author adequately describes the need to be alert and agile in our approach to children's new play patterns: 'we must always be receptive to new forms of interplay; and we must always come back to the children and learn to recognise the signs of unknown resources which yet might flourish'. I propose that a new kind of play is emerging and the signs are evidenced primarily in and around screen-based play.

A young child's attention and involvement in screen play

Interestingly, Marsh (2010a) suggests that rather than 'pinning down definitions' locating signals associated with different kinds of play might be useful. Play discourse is at the intersection of several disciplines and, as such, the notion of play is difficult to define. My particular research interest lies within a narrow field: a young child's attention and involvement in screen play and its contribution to a creative experience as described by flow and autotelic experiences. Nevertheless, as screens demand a high level of visual literacy, this has much to contribute to the discussion. But first, there is a need to provide a brief analysis of continuities and discontinuities between historical theories of play and play in general media. Consequently, I draw on Brian Sutton-Smith's work *The Ambiguity of Play* (2001), which discusses seven rhetorics of play which usefully draw together conceptualizations of play, suggesting that across the different disciplines each bring into being rhetorics for specific purposes for play. For example, the notion of *play as progress* leads Sutton-Smith to suggest that play can be viewed as developmental growth and hence he draws upon the disciplines of biology, education and psychology. Again, he addresses the notion of play as fate (magic and luck) and the act of the imagination being attributed to other disciplines such as art and literature and the creativity agenda. Returning to the work of Marsh, the suggestion that play today (within media) can usefully be apportioned to either continuities or discontinuities is a clear approach to take. Thus, continuities in play over time appear to lie in the areas of the functions of play: having fun, distraction from boredom, coming to terms with emotional challenges, play as a way of letting off steam, pretend play etc. Further, continuities can be located in terms of 'framing' – how children frame or position the meaning of their play.

The discontinuities in play can be described in the area of the more complicated ways in which children can now link globally and locally through new media assemblages. These extend to new kinds of texts as there are now different modalities which are breaking down boundaries between the online and offline world (Marsh, 2010b). In very much the same way, boundaries between adult and child play are now being dissolved as both tend to inhabit the same media space (for older children, Facebook for example and video game practice). I suggest that multimodal practice alongside portability and the capacity to rewind and replay content, all contribute to the ways in which play today is impacted. As Kinder (1993) suggests, 'transmedia' enables the use of wider artefacts in tying them to new narratives and then being able to take the experience with them via tablets and smartphones. The barrier between online and offline play is being eroded. Of course, iTunes, apps and tablets promote cross consumption of the other and children can even copy media texts in taking film narrative into other areas and embedding the dialogue. I propose that they collect together strands from other play patterns into the fabric of play in the digital world.

The never-ending feature of play provides a point of difference in the new media play. The narrative need never finish! This new kind of play is immersive, taking the very essence of the state of flow as described by Csikszentmihalyi (1991) and embodying it within interactions with digital media (Harding, 2015).

Future developments in digital media are highlighting this feature as fundamental, for example, through QR codes and wearable technologies (pyjamas with QR codes for bedtime stories).

It is notable that with each of the descriptive elements concerning play there were numerous features that were apparent in this new kind of digital play, but none of the identified types of play completely satisfied that which I was witnessing. Most importantly, I am positioning the child as an active agent in the process insofar as they are transferring play practices by utilising their representations from traditional methods of play; they are using the same meta-messages but representing them differently. In the 2014 small-scale study referenced above, 85 per cent of those surveyed in the two to five age range believed that children are active not passive participants in the media they use. Consequently we are witnessing a new kind of playful media experience: digital symbolic representative play that warrants the closest of examination. Hodge and Tripp (1986) discussed children's highly literate states when it comes to understanding representational codes of TV and called upon educationalists and parents to take this area of their lives more seriously and contest the traditional understanding of literacy.

Schemas and digital play

Most significantly, when studying a young child's navigation across multimodal literacies, I began to observe a pattern: these gestures and signs which children are viewing on screen appear to be the ones to which children pay the most attention and show greater levels of engagement and involvement. The gestures and signs fell neatly into the area of schematic movements. The relationship between schemas and how children are attracted to schematic movements on screen became my next step of enquiry. Tina Bruce (1997) in Harding (2013), proposes that schemas are a cluster of pieces that fit together. Furthermore, she describes schemas as behaviours, which the child can utilise in varying ways in different places and situations. This supports the understanding that the young child can hold a mental image of a favoured schematic movement, and I suggest, even transferring this recognition to an on-screen movement. Indeed, Vygotsky describes how movement precedes perception: the child resolves her choice not through the direct process of visual perception but through movement (1978: 34).

I began to pilot test the possibility that children might recognise schemas through a screen-based narrative, which focused, for example, on the trajectory schema. Subsequently, I produced a pilot TV show which drew on schemas as woven into the fabric of the narrative and built on the responses from the children observed. Immediately, the children made the connection between schemas they had recognised in a real situation to the one spoken about in the story and the one that they had seen on screen where real children were involved in the same schematic movements. In fact, Athey in *Extending Thought in Young Children* (2008: 197) comments that while watching a cartoon, one child said: 'They're all dizzy.' She had noticed the effect of rotation. Although, clearly Athey was not researching the impact of schema recognition on screen, nevertheless, this was pertinent and interesting to my work. The TV show was then developed further into an animation and live action promo and was also tested. The recognition and fascination of schematic movements on screen yielded similar results. The levels of attention and engagement were high on the engagement and involvement scale that was previously developed (Harding, 2015).

Facilitating this new digital image-based play

Perhaps redefining conventional definitions of childhood through social usage rather than in terms of biological age is helpful. The argument follows that 'adulthood' and 'childhood' no longer occupy a traditional normative space in terms of media practice (Buckingham, 1994). Undoubtedly, this discourse is inseparable from specific social, cultural and historical circumstances.

It's a power struggle

Policy discourse which concerns involving children in decisions regarding media is set within the framework of the UN Conventions of the Rights of the Child (Messenger Davies, 2010). Article 13 concerns the child's right 'to seek, receive, and impart information and ideas of all kinds, regardless of frontiers, either orally, in writing or in print, in the form of art, or through any other media of the child's choice'. I propose that the practical solution to this edict lies within the power of digital content providers through the offering of a more participatory role with young children.

In the small-scale study (2014) as previously discussed, parents and educators across the age range tended to suggest a similar range of strategies: 'quality; appropriate; guide them; be aware of safety; understand it well yourself; get a balance'. Furthermore, scores were particularly interesting in the two to seven years age range, where children were considered by parents to be 'very independent' when playing with a variety of media devices.

DISCUSSION TOPICS

- Discuss the following statement with a colleague: 'All new media platforms offer children the same level of engagement and involvement.'
- Share a holiday photograph with a colleague and decide whether in the absence of the photograph, words better describe the scene.
- Choose a popular children's website. How many entry points can be identified? Make a direct comparison with a tablet application for a story and then a child's traditional storybook. What are the differences? Establish the benefits of entry points.
- 'Children are meaning-makers set to make new discoveries in digital symbolic representation: early years educators are ill equipped to assist them in this task.' Discuss this statement.

Conclusion

In summary, the power of the image to engage and satisfy the curiosity of the young child is undeniable. The position and relationship between text and image is shifting simultaneously, demanding a paradigm shift in adult mindset. Children are well-positioned to integrate the use of their senses to decode meaning and are, I propose, in a sense ahead of the game in their flexibility of thought. In the small-scale study, the adults testified to the powerful draw of images and the active involvement they appeared to demand. There was almost unanimous agreement among the adults surveyed that there should be full exploitation of the attraction that images produce and at the same time a prevailing sense that adults must familiarise themselves with the digital landscape in order to become efficient mentors. It's an exciting time for digital representation and the search for the power of digital symbolic representation has only just begun.

References

Athey, C. (2008). *Extending Thought in Young Children*, 2nd edn. London: Paul Chapman Publishing.

Bazalgette, C. (1991). *Media Education*. London: Hodder & Stoughton.

Bruner, J. S., Jolly, A. and Sylva, K. (eds) (1976). *Play – It's Role Development and Evolution*. London: Penguin.

Buckingham, D. (1994). *Children Talking Television: The Making of Television Literacy*. London: Routledge.

Buckingham, D. (1996). *Moving Images*. Manchester: Manchester University Press.

Buckingham, D. (2003). *Media Education: Literacy, Learning and Contemporary Culture*. Cambridge: Polity Press.

Csikszentmihalyi, M. (1991). *Flow: The Psychology of Optimal Experience*. London: Harper Collins.

Donaldson, M. (1986). *Children's Minds*. London: Fontana Press.

Fox, C. (1993). *At the Very Edge of the Forest: The Influence of Literature on Storytelling*. London: Cassell.

Harding, J. (2013). *Child Development*. London: Hodder.

Harding, J. (2015). *The Development of a Pilot Tool for Examining Engagement and Involvement in Screen-Based Activities in the Early Years*. PhD thesis, Middlesex University.

Hodge, R. and Tripp, D. (1986). *Children and Television: A Semiotic Approach*. Cambridge: Polity Press.

Kinder, M. (1993). *Playing with Power in Movies, Television, and Video Games: From Muppet Babies to Teenage Mutant Ninja Turtles*. Berkeley, CA: University of California Press.

Kress, G. (2003). *Literacy in the New Media Age*. London: Routledge.

Marsh, J. (2003). Contemporary models of communicative practice: Shaky foundations in the Foundation Stage? *English in Education*, 37(1): 38–46.

Marsh, J. (ed.) (2005). *Popular Culture, New Media and Digital Literacy in Early Childhood*. London: RoutledgeFalmer.

Marsh, J. (2010a). *Childhood, Culture and Creativity: A Literature Review*. Newcastle: Creativity, Culture and Education.

Marsh, J. (2010b). Young children's play in online virtual worlds. *Journal of Early Childhood Research*, 8(1): 23–39.

Marsh, J. and Hallet, E. (eds) (2010). *Desirable Literacies: Approaches to Language and Literacy in the Early Years*. London: Sage.

Marsh, J., Brooks, G., Hughes, J., Ritchie, L. and Roberts, S. (2005). *Digital Beginnings. Young Children's Use of Popular Culture, Media and New Technologies*. Sheffield: University of Sheffield.

McGonigal, J. (2012). *Reality is Broken*. London: Vintage.

Messenger Davies, M. (2010). *Children, Media and Culture*. Berkshire: Open University Press.

Parker, D. (2006). Making it move, making it mean: Animation, print literacy and the metafunctions of language. In J. Marsh and E. Millard (eds), *Popular Literacies, Childhood and Schooling*. London: Routledge.

Saussure, F. (1986 [1916]). *Course in General Linguistics*. New York: Open Court.

Sutton-Smith, B. (2001). *The Ambiguity of Play*. London: Harvard University Press.

Vygotsky, L. (1978). *Mind in Society: The Development of Higher Psychological Processes* (eds. M. Cole, V. John-Stiner, S. Scribner and E. Souberman). London: Havard University Press.

State of play

Technology in the early years curriculum

Lorraine Kaye

Introduction

Since the establishment of the first nursery school there have been a vast number of developments in early childhood education both nationally and internationally. The recognition, during the seventeenth century, that early years had a positive and important role to play in human development was led by many European philosophers and educators such as Jan Amos Comenius, Jean-Jacques Rousseau and Johann Pestalozzi. They believed in the importance of first-hand experience, learning through play, and the impact of positive reinforcement and active learning during early childhood. In 1816, Robert Owen established the first nursery school, in Scotland, set up for the children of his cotton mill workers from the age of one. A German educator, Friedrich Froebel (1782–1852), started a school for children and named it 'Kindergarten'; he believed strongly in learning through play. The trend was continued by Maria Montessori (1869–1952), who emphasised the individual over class teaching, where children are given liberty to follow self-chosen activities.

During and after the Second World War, the influence on early childhood practice was very much based on the theories of Froebel, Montessori and Steiner (1865–1925) and public policy towards early childhood education evolved as a result of demand for an enriching pre-school education for a growing middle class, helping meet the needs of working mothers and preparing children for primary schooling. From the 1980s the emphasis shifted from child development to the sociocultural contexts of childhood learning (Dahlberg *et al.*, 1999 in Bruce, 2005) and the integration of both biological and sociocultural strands is considered in current practice (Bruce, 2005).

However, current developments in early childhood education and their curricula seem to have neglected to take account of the advances in technology and the current digital society in which young children live. This chapter aims to address the place of technology in early years curricula in general and in relation to the changes to the curriculum for computing in primary education in England. Additionally, it will consider ways in which technology can and should be incorporated into an early years curriculum.

Play and technology in early childhood curricula

In her 2013 article, 'Digital play in the early years', Susan Edwards writes,

> "The separation of play and technologies in early childhood curriculum documents persists despite rapid advances in the pace of digitisation in post-industrial societies (Hobbs, 2010) and the consequent need for young children to develop 'new' skills in reading, navigating and participating in highly digitally-mediated environments (Bittman et al., 2011)."
>
> (Edwards, 2013: 201).

There is, therefore, a need to consider how this disparity can be addressed within an early year's curriculum in order to include the use of technology as an important part of children's play to reflect the digital world in which they are operating.

Edwards (2013) argues this separation of children's play and their use of technology exists in early years curriculum in a number of countries. She cites Aotearoa New Zealand's *Te Whāriki Early Childhood Curriculum* (Ministry of Education, 1996), and Sweden's *Curriculum for the Preschool* (Skolverket: Swedish National Agency for Education, 2010) as examples of curricula that discuss play as essential for supporting children's learning.

> "In these documents technologies are listed separately from descriptions of children's play and are described as learning outcomes or useful tools for supporting children's communication skills and/or creative outputs. [...] technologies are not identified as relevant to the provision of early childhood curricula at all."
>
> (Edwards, 2013: 200-201)

Edwards (2013) also notes the National Association of the Education for Young Children (NAEYC) the leading professional association in the USA, made no mention at all of the use of digital technology in their publication, *Developmentally Appropriate Practice Guidelines for Practice* (National Association of the Education for Young Children, 2009). Interestingly, this was revised by the NAEYC in 2012 and their current website considers the role of technology and includes recommendations for effective classroom practice for children from birth to age eight.

The NAEYC's key points for the use of technology tools and interactive media for pre-school and kindergarten children are listed in Figure 5.1.

A curriculum for early childhood is 'integrally tied to a concern for dealing comprehensively with "the whole child", the child's physical, social, cognitive, and emotional development' (Essa, 1999: 206). Few children enter early childhood education unaware of the use of technology both at home and in their wider environment.

- Allow children to freely explore touchscreens loaded with a wide variety of developmentally appropriate interactive media experiences that are well designed and enhance feelings of success.
- Provide opportunities for children to begin to explore and feel comfortable using 'traditional' mouse and keyboard computers to use Websites or look up answers with a search engine.
- Capture photos of block buildings or artwork that children have created; videotape dramatic play to replay for children.
- Celebrate children's accomplishments with digital media displayed on a digital projector or on a classroom Website.
- Incorporate assistive technologies as appropriate for children with special needs and/or developmental delays.
- Record children's stories about their drawings or their play; make digital audio or video files to document their progress.
- Explore digital story-telling with children. Co-create digital books with photos of the children's play or work; attach digital audio files with the child as the narrator.

Source: NAEYC, 2012

FIGURE 5.1 Technology tools and interactive media.

Digital experiences in home and school contexts

The impact of technological developments have had a considerable effect on the lives of young children who are as engaged in the social practices of the 'new media age' (Kress, 2003) as the older children, adolescents and adults who surround them (Marsh et al., 2005; Plowman et al., 2012). Within this technological age, many young children develop a wide range of skills, knowledge and understanding of this world. They often refer to an *iPad* for information and pleasure; they are familiar with the internet and smartphones being used for various forms of interactions on a daily basis (Plowman et al., 2010). A major influence on children's technology usage therefore is imitation of significant adults, whom they see using these devices. Young children often do aspire to be like the adults in their life and it is understandable why they would want to use similar technology and as often as they do (*New York Daily News*, online). Family members, be they parents, siblings or other close relations, develop children's understanding of the technological tools around them and in society. This may either be by direct instruction or implicitly through observation of their use.

In research studies by Marsh (in Yelland, 2005) on the way in which popular and media texts inform children's communicative practices, she extended Cairney and Ruge's typology of uses of literacy in homes in identifying several key purposes for literacy in the home context.

Table 5.1 demonstrates how many children develop a sense of themselves through the media – they use the media to perform different identities and try out new roles with reference to their favourite sociocultural worlds, linked to popular media prevalent in their world, be it texts (printed and online), television programmes and/ or computer programs/games.

TABLE 5.1 Classifications of communicative practices related to popular culture and media and examples of home practices in each category

Communicative practices	Examples
For forming social relationships	• Playing console-based computer games with fathers and siblings • Watching television and films with family members • Reading print-based texts with family members, e.g. picture books related to television and popular culture, TV guides, catalogues, magazines • Using toy mobile phones to talk to family members; watching family members send SMS text messages
For development of skills, knowledge and understanding in relation to language and literacy	• Developing vocabulary and phoneme–grapheme correspondence from watching television • Developing skills in relation to (popular) computer-game playing, e.g. hand–eye coordination, problem-solving, parallel-processing • Developing specific skills related to educative PC computer games • Developing oral language through media-related play • Interacting with comics and popular games focused on skills development
For accessing or displaying information	• Reading junk mail/catalogues/computer game covers and magazines • Reading teletext on satellite television • Reading TV guide • Accessing websites on internet (e.g. BBC children's sites)
For pleasure and enjoyment	• Watching television programmes, cartoons and films • Playing computer games • Playing with toys and artefacts related to popular cultural narratives
For identity construction and performance of self	• Playing related to narratives accessed in a variety of modes • Playing with toys and artefacts which were part of the narrativised semiotic system formed by popular cultural and media texts

Source: Marsh (2005) after Cairney and Ruge (1998).

Studies that have explored relationships between home and school literacies have highlighted discontinuities and tensions in relation to the use of new technologies. McTavish's (2009) case study of eight-year-old Rajan exemplifies how children may differentiate between literacy practices at home and school: while Rajan's school-based practices were book-based, individual and print orientated, his home-based practices were multilingual and often associated with networked, multimodal texts embedded in meaningful, social contexts.

As Knobel (2006) points out:

> Valuing and utilising children's out-of-school practices are not just about engaging them in classrooms, however. It also offers recognition of the new kinds of learning they are undertaking outside school and accepts that some of these emerging skills, knowledge and understanding need to be developed further in an educational environment.

(Marsh *et al.*, 2005: 12)

Technology in the current Early Years Statutory Framework in England

The use of technology was introduced into England's early years curriculum in the late 1990s with the publication of the DfEE guidance, *Nursery Education: Desirable Outcomes for Children's Learning on Entering Compulsory Education* (SCAA, 1996). However, technology at that time was seen purely as a tool which children could use, where appropriate, to support their learning. It was the curriculum guidance of 2000 that introduced the requirement that children were to actually learn about the technology itself in that they were to 'find out about and identify the uses of everyday technology' (DfEE, 2000). It was then, as it still is now, incumbent upon practitioners to interpret the Early Learning Goal so that it provided challenges to children growing up in an increasingly technological world.

The revised curriculum in 2012 made little change. Computing and IT is outlined in the specific area of 'Understanding the World' which involves guiding children to make sense of their physical world and their community through opportunities to explore, observe and find out about people, places, technology and the environment. The current Early Learning Goal also demands that children recognise that a range of technology is used in places such as homes and schools and that they select and use technology for particular purposes (DfE, 2012). The focus on children using a computer in ICT has been broadened. This is to reflect the fact that through continuing developments in technology young children are often conversant with a broader range of applications and technological devices than in previous decades. However, it fails to make explicit whether it is the practitioner or the children that have determined the purpose for which the technology is to be used. A challenging and appropriate interpretation of this goal would be to insist that children can only achieve the goal when they can select appropriate technologies and use them to fulfil a purpose of their own conception.

Development Matters in the Early Years Foundation Stage (EYFS) is non-statutory guidance material which supports practitioners in implementing the statutory requirements of the EYFS. This provides further explanation of the interconnection between the overarching principles of the Framework (see Chapter 8), the characteristics of effective learning, and the prime and specific areas of learning and development – see Figure 5.2 below.

It can be seen that the characteristics of effective teaching and learning are central to the Early Years Framework, which states that:

> in planning and guiding children's activities, practitioners must reflect on the different ways that children learn and reflect these in their practice. The three characteristics of effective teaching and learning are:
>
> ■ playing and exploring – children investigate and experience things, and 'have a go';
>
> ■ active learning – children concentrate and keep on trying if they encounter difficulties, and enjoy achievements; and
>
> ■ creating and thinking critically – children have and develop their own ideas, make links between ideas, and develop strategies for doing things.
>
> (DfE, 2013: 1.9)

The characteristics of effective learning and the prime and specific areas of learning and development are all interconnected.

- The ways in which the child engages with other people and their environment – playing and exploring, active learning, and creating and thinking critically – underpin learning and development across all areas and support the child to remain an effective and motivated learner.

- The **prime** areas begin to develop quickly in response to relationships and experiences, and run through and support learning in all other areas. The prime areas continue to be fundamental throughout the EYFS.

- The **specific** areas include essential skills and knowledge. They grow out of the prime areas, and provide important contexts for learning.

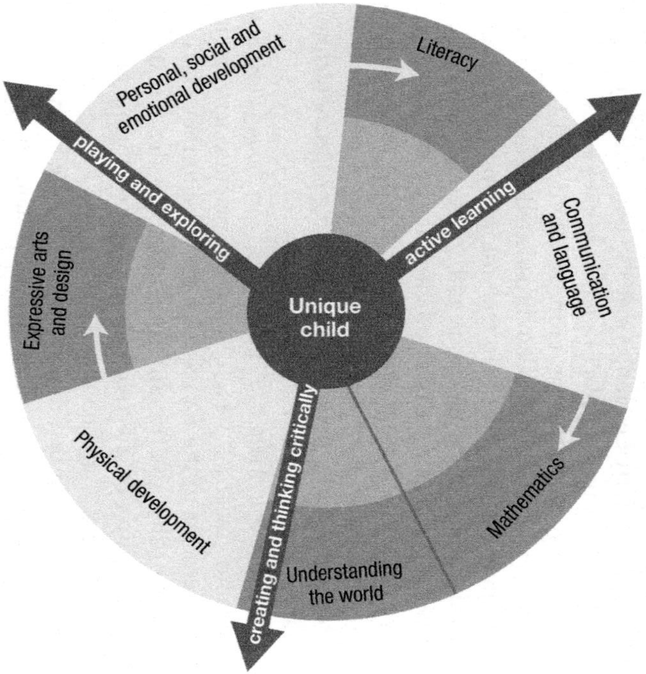

Prime areas are fundamental, work together, and move through to support development in all other areas.
- Personal, social and emotional development
- Communication and language
- Physical development

Specific areas include essential skills and knowledge for children to participate successfully in society.
- Literacy
- Mathematics
- Understanding the world
- Expressive arts and design

The Unique Child reaches out to relate to people and things through the **Characteristics of Effective Learning,** which move through all areas of learning.
- playing and exploring
- active learning
- creating and thinking critically

Children develop in the context of relationships and the environment around them.

This is unique to each family, and reflects individual communities and cultures.

Communication and language

Literacy

active learning

Mathematics

Unique child

Understanding the world

creating and thinking critically

personal, social and emotional development

playing and exploring

Expressive arts and design

Physical development

FIGURE 5.2 An adaption of Early Education (2012). *Development Matters in the Early Years Foundation Stage* (EYFS).

In considering the characteristics of effective learning, many of these can be seen in young children's use of technological tools; evident relationships to the statements in *Development Matters* are outlined in Table 5.2. The original table has been annotated to include examples of tools and activities that could be used to demonstrate some of the stated characteristics of effective learning (see reflection topics at the end of the chapter for a related task).

TABLE 5.2 EYFS Development Matters: Characteristics of effective learning and the use of computer tools

Playing and Exploring: engagement

Finding out and exploring

Engaging in open-ended activity

Being willing to 'have a go'

- Taking a risk, engaging in new experiences, and learning by trial and error

Using an appropriate program or website

Active Learning: motivation

Keeping on trying

- Persisting with activity when challenges occur
- Showing a belief that more effort or a different approach will pay off
- Bouncing back after difficulties

Enjoying achieving what they set out to do

- Showing satisfaction in meeting their own goals
- Being proud of how they accomplished something – not just the end result

Creating and thinking critically: thinking

Having their own ideas

- Thinking of ideas
- Finding ways to solve problems
- Finding new ways to do things

Using a range of tools in a painting program, e.g. spray paint, rainbow paint

Making links

- Making links and noticing patterns in their experience
- Making predictions
- Testing their ideas
- Developing ideas of grouping, sequences, cause and effect

Activity using a programmable toy such as Bee-Bot®

Choosing ways to do things

- Planning, making decisions about how to approach a task, solve a problem and reach a goal
- Checking how well their activities are going
- Changing strategy as needed
- Reviewing how well the approach worked

Developments in the primary curriculum in England for computing

As children reach the end of Foundation Stage (aged five years), the curriculum which they need to follow is the Primary National Curriculum in England Key Stages 1 and 2 Framework Document covering ages seven to eleven years. In her review of the Early Years Foundation Stage prior to the publication of the current Early Years Statutory Framework, Tickell (2011) observed,

> One of the key pressures that people highlighted was the perceived disconnect between the EYFS and Key Stage 1. I believe that more could be done to ensure stronger links between the EYFS and the National Curriculum ... I am aware that the National Curriculum is currently under review, and I encourage the Government to ensure that this join up is sustained when the new National Curriculum is launched. The transition between the EYFS and Year 1 should be seamless.
>
> (Tickell, 2011: 11)

The recent revision to the primary curriculum for computing (DfE, 2013) will therefore be examined in further detail.

In July 2010, the Minister for Culture, Communications and the Creative Industries commissioned a review of the skills needs of the UK's video games and visual effects industries. This review set in motion a chain reaction which resulted in Michael Gove, the Secretary of State for Education, declaring in January 2012 that 'we have a problem with our current ICT curriculum' (Gove, 2012).

In 2011, several organisations became actively involved in promoting improvements in UK computing education (Neil *et al.*, 2013). Additionally, the highly influential Nesta *Next Gen* report (Livingstone, 2011) was published, which highlighted the skills and pathways required to support the UK's digital/creative industries and contended that computer science should be a core part of the school curriculum (Brown *et al.*, 2014). This was supported by the industry, including a widely publicised speech by Google's executive chairman:

> I was flabbergasted to learn that today computer science isn't even taught as standard in UK schools ... Your IT curriculum focuses on teaching how to use software, but gives no insight into how it's made.
>
> (Schmidt, 2011, cited in Brown *et al.*, 2014)

The outcome was a demand by the Government for a computing curriculum at Key Stages 1–3 as a replacement for the Information and Communications Technology (ICT) curriculum. Not surprisingly this has resulted in a very significant change in emphasis in the curriculum. At Key Stage 1 this states that pupils should be taught to:

- understand what algorithms are, how they are implemented as programs on digital devices, and that programs execute by following precise and unambiguous instructions;
- create and debug simple programs;
- use logical reasoning to predict the behaviour of simple programs;

- use technology purposefully to create, organise, store, manipulate and retrieve digital content;
- use technology safely and respectfully, keeping personal information private, and know where to go for help and support when they have concerns about material on the internet;
- recognise common uses of information technology beyond school.

(DfE, 2013)

One of the consequences of the change of emphasis to include computer science in the primary curriculum is that many primary teachers will need training to update their knowledge and skills in computer programming. There are initiatives to support this training. For example, Computing in Schools (CAS) offer free computer science training for primary teachers who will then be able to support other teachers within their Network of Teaching Excellence in Computer Science schools (CAS, online). In addition, Microsoft is implementing a new training program designed to help primary school teachers prepare for the revised computing curriculum (ITProPortal, online).

It is very apparent that the current early years guidance was published prior to the conception of a computing curriculum. Consequently there is now potential for a marked discontinuity between the received curriculum in the Early Years Foundation Stage and that in Key Stage 1. Schools need to consider this potential discontinuity and make decisions about whether they will make any changes to their early years curriculum to lessen any negative effect it could have on their children's learning, or alternatively whether they will leave the early years curriculum as it is and introduce the computing curriculum at Key Stage 1.

Incorporating technology in an early years curriculum

Key issues/challenges

As evidenced in other chapters of this book, current research has identified multiple benefits of the use of technology by young children. These include:

- facilitating cognitive development;
- enhancing creative thinking and problem-solving skills;
- improving social interaction and language.

It is not suggested that the use of technology should replace current, valued practice involving activities using blocks, sand, water, art, dramatic play, outdoor play, books, emergent writing activities, etc. Rather, the technological tools *supplement* the children's learning and development. The challenge then for many early years settings is the integration of technological tools into their curriculum and planning in order to maximise the benefits.

A further challenge is the ongoing debate over the place of technology in children's lives (see Chapter 1), which may lead to some confusion and questioning of practitioners' beliefs in the use of technology in early years education: '[The] mismatch in advice from research and major organizations may lead to more insecurity over using technology with young children, which then could impact teachers' actual use' (Blackwell *et al.*, 2013). In order to support early years educators, a technology policy is needed that sets out how to incorporate technology appropriately into their curriculum to meet the developmental needs of young children.

Key principles

The use of multimedia tools is entirely compatible with the open-ended, non-linear, constructivist model of learning (see Chapter 1). The technologies allow teachers and children to create interactive lessons, presentations and projects through the integration of images, graphics, text, animation, audio and motion video. Learning is enhanced by communication, resulting in new knowledge, re-organized knowledge or additional understanding, with groups of children learning how to use the tools of their culture in a collaborative learning environment (Cox and Cox, 2009).

The following principles arose from the Kidsmart project (Siraj-Blatchford *et al.*, 2001) and are still relevant in relation to the appropriate use of technology in early years education:

1   Ensure an educational purpose
■   Can the technology be planned into areas of learning?
2   Encourage collaboration
■   Think about your computer setup, for example two chairs, with tablets on a table? Does the application encourage social play?
3   Integrate with other aspects of the curriculum
■   As a tool for learning
4   Ensure the child is in control
■   Can the child control the technology or is it the other way around?
5   Choose applications that are transparent
■   How user friendly is it? What does someone need to know in order to get the best from it? Can this be broken down easily?
6   Avoid applications containing violence or stereotyping
7   Be aware of health and safety issues
■   Small mouse, monitors at right angle and height, large buttons on camera, etc.
Parental involvement should also go hand-in-hand with these.

(Siraj-Blatchford *et al.*, 2001)

Early years educators should also be aware of the stages of development towards using a piece of equipment, software or website in order to provide support and to extend children's learning and development. These are based on Piaget's stages of cognitive development (Piaget, 1971):

Stimulated by
■   Should be enjoyable and stimulating; what happens and how.

Explore

■ Provide lots of opportunities to explore in order to gain the relevant knowledge and skills and gain a sense of control.

Practice

■ Provide opportunities to put into practice what they know. Observe and talk through this practice with children and scaffold their learning.

Use for an intended purpose

■ Children begin to use the software for an intended purpose; model different uses of the software.

In fact, many of us go through similar stages ourselves when faced with a new program or technological tool.

Implementation

McManis and Gunnewig (2012) suggest that new digital tools, such as smart mobile devices and their accompanying applications, can offer unique opportunities for young children to participate in useful and targeted activities. Using embedded cameras in such tools to take photographs or video of the world around them, young children are able to create texts and narrative structures connected to their own interests and their own lives and that present purposeful uses of literacy aimed at real audiences. They provide opportunities for children to create, modify and use their own multimodal texts in multiple ways, and to share in collective endeavours (Laidlaw and O'Mara, 2011).

If, for example, children are learning about their environment, they may explore the outdoor area, local park, local shops, etc. The use of a tablet or a digital camera, *by the children*, may help recall their trip and support discussion and related activities back in the classroom. This may include a sequence of the trip and/or taking photographs of items found in the environment. It is important, therefore, that before the trip, the children know exactly how to operate the digital device they will be using, including how to take pictures and how to delete them. Without these skills the time will be spent on supporting children to use the camera rather than on exploring and observing the environment they are in.

Video-conferencing resources can also help provide authentic experiences to assist young children researching answers to enquiry questions. If children are especially interested in dinosaurs, for example, practitioners can support children in connecting to experts at the Natural History Museum (www.nhm.ac.uk). Video-conferencing applications also provide the opportunity to communicate with children around the world to share experiences and develop their understanding of other cultures.

Early years settings with an interactive whiteboard allow children to explain and extend their thinking across all areas of learning and development through the use of resources which include open-ended questions and discussion opportunities for shared thinking. The interactive whiteboard can enhance children's learning by 'allowing children to engage positively in imaginative, active and social learning' and by 'offering a visual means for demonstrating and exemplifying ... involve[ing] children in watching, listening, doing, constructing and creating' (Price, online). Additionally, embedding technology in an early years curriculum can provide a vital connection to family members and the wider community. The maintenance of a blog or website provides the opportunity for children to share their learning and their experiences with friends and family – at home and abroad. It can also provide important information for parents, carers and the community about events, learning activities and celebrations. There are numerous examples of early years centres which have successfully embedded technology throughout their curriculum, such as Hampden Way Nursery (www.hampdenway.barnet.sch.uk) and Gamesley Early Excellence Centre (www.gamesleyeec.org.uk) and whose websites provide examples and suggestions of the integration of technology. The most significant factor found in the successful integration of technology in these early years centres was the belief, understanding and commitment by the practitioners of the potential benefits and relevance of the use of technology to support, enhance and extend children's learning and development in a digital age.

The following questions may help identify how to integrate these tools into an early years curriculum:

■ How much experience do the children have with the chosen technology?

■ How will I organise this activity: whole or small group?

■ How does this experience connect to my goals and objectives for this unit or topic?

■ What is the social-emotional context and skills linked to this activity?

■ How will this experience inform future planning?

(Puerling, online)

Figure 5.3 provides an example of planning for the use of a range of technological tools across the curriculum within a topic. This includes suggestions for both content-based and content-free (general purpose such as a word processor) software, relevant websites and other non-computer based resources.

DISCUSSION TOPICS

■ Consider a range of technological tools and activities which could be used to demonstrate the characteristics outlined in Table 5.2.

■ How can continuity be ensured in children's learning about technology when the early years curriculum and the Key Stage 1 curriculum have different foci?

■ Should practitioners plan and deliver an early years curriculum that will prepare children for the demands of the Key Stage 1 computing curriculum?

	PRIME				SPECIFIC		
ICT resources	Communication and language	Personal, social and emotional development	Physical development	Literacy	Mathematical development	Expressive arts and design	Understanding of the World
Content-based software		**Create a story** – write a story about their day		Using **Clicker6** to write a story about your interests		Using **2paint** to make a self-portrait	**2City** – create scenes from your home town and what you like to do
Content-free software	Using a word processor to write a letter to a family member, talking about what you want to be when you're older		Using a word processor to write what is similar and what is different from then and now		Using the interactive whiteboard to make a Venn diagram including names of everybody in the class, choose a category and get them to slide their names into the relevant category	Using a drawing program to draw a picture of your house	
WWW	Get some possible job ideas from: www.youtube.com/ watch?v=j4S8LnHzuuE	Build your Wild Self: www.buildyourwildself. com/		Using: www.bbc.co.uk/ cbeebies/games/ time-for-school-my-school-book A book about your first day at school			Using: www.getinthezone.org.uk/ schools/ages-4-11/ ages-4-5/game-brilliant-bodies/ Use this link to get children to play the game, naming parts of the body
Non-computer resources, e.g. tape recorder	Use **easy speak microphones** to record three facts that we may not know about them	Bring in pictures of different possible jobs, e.g. police officer, nurse, postman/woman	Bring in a photo of when you were a baby and now	Bring in five items that most relate to you, and use these to write a story			Image of the human body with labelled parts, to show the class before they play the game

FIGURE 5.3 Example Plan: Foundation Stage theme: 'All about me'.
Source: Kaye, 2015.

Conclusion

Abbott (2001) suggests that 'most educational systems do not respond quickly to technological advances' and almost fifteen years later, this is still the case. Early years educators are reluctant to use the digital tools of a technological age without evidence of its benefit to young children's development and without clear guidance. Changing policy will be critical to redefining developmentally appropriate technology use in an early years curriculum. However, standards, assessment and funding play an important role in communicating information to early childhood education providers and in the development of an early years curriculum (Daugherty *et al.*, 2014).

As House *et al.* (2012) succinctly put it:

> In the current highly uncertain political and cultural climate, early years development and learning that focuses on sustainable living and learning is necessary more than it has ever been. This in turn requires different, creative and critical approaches to early years experiences that consider the actualities of the world in which children live, and the best ways to create learning milieux that attend to these realities.
>
> (House *et al.*, 2012)

References

Abbott, C. (2001). *ICT: Changing Education*. London: RoutledgeFalmer.

Bittman, M., Rutherford, L., Brown, J. and Unsworth, L. (2011). Digital natives? New and old media and children's outcomes. *Australian Journal of Education*, 55(2): 161–175.

Blackwell, C. K., Lauricella, A. R., Wartella, E., Robb, M. and Schomburg, R. (2013). Adoption and use of technology in early education. *Computers and Education,* 69: 310.

Brown, N. C. C., Sentance, S., Crick, T. and Humphreys, S. (2014). Restart: The resurgence of computer science in UK schools. *ACM Trans. Comput. Educ.* 14(2), Article 9. DOI: http://dx.doi.org/10.1145/2602484

Bruce, T. (2005). *Early Childhood Education*. London: Hodder Arnold.

Cairney, T. H. and Ruge, J. (1998). *Community Literacy Practices and Schooling: Towards Effective Support for Students* (Vols 1 and 2). Canberra: DEETYA.

Computing at School: www.computingatschool.org.uk (accessed November 2015).

Cox, J. and Cox, K. (2009). Constructivism and integrating technology in the classroom. www.icgiovanni23esimo.gov.it/wp/wp-content/uploads/2015/01/CONSTRUCTIVISM-AND-INTEGRATING-TECHNOLOGY-IN-THE-CLASSROOM.pdf (accessed April 2016).

Daugherty, L., Dossani, R., Johnson, E.-E. and Wright, C. (2014). *Moving Beyond Screen Time: Redefining Developmentally Appropriate Technology Use in Early Childhood Education*. Santa Monica, CA: RAND Corporation. www.rand.org/pubs/research_reports/RR673z2 (accessed October 2015).

DfE (2012). *Statutory Framework for the Early Years Foundation Stage*. Runcorn: Department for Education.

DfE (2013). *The National Curriculum in England: Key Stages 1 and 2 Framework Document*. www.gov.uk/government/publications/national-curriculum-in-england-primary-curriculum (accessed July 2014).

DfEE (2000). *Curriculum Guidance for the Foundation Stage*. London: Department for Education.

Early Education (2012). *Development Matters in the Early Years Foundation Stage (EYFS)*. London: Early Education.

Edwards, S. (2013). Digital play in the early years: A contextual response to the problem of integrating digital technologies and play-based learning in the early childhood curriculum. *European Early Childhood Education Research Journal*, 21(2), 199–212.

Essa, E. (1999). *Introduction to Early Childhood Education*. Albany, NY: Delmar.

Gove, M. (2012). Michael Gove speech at BETT Show 2012. January 2012. London: DfE. www.gov. uk/government/speeches/michael-gove-speech-at-the-bett-show-2012 (accessed November 2014).

Hobbs, R. (2010). *Digital Media and Literacy: A Plan of Action. A White Paper on the Digital and Media Literacy Recommendations of the Knight Commission on the Information Needs of Communities in a Democracy.* Washington: The Aspen Institute.

House, R., Osgood, J. and Simpson, K. (2012). *Unhurried Pathways: A New Framework for Early Childhood.* Early Childhood Action. www.earlychildhoodaction.com/docs/ECA%20 EYF%20Unhurried%20Pathways.pdf (accessed October 2015).

ITProPortal: www.itproportal.com/2014/01/20/microsoft-training-160000-primary-school-teachers-computing-ahead-curriculum-change/#ixzz3qMQ595qc (accessed March 2016).

Kaye, L. (2015). Planning, teaching and assessing computing lessons. Lecture to BA Primary Education, EDP 1213 An Introduction to Computing and Technology. Middlesex University, 21 March 2015.

Knobel, M. (2006). Technokids, Koala Trouble and *Pokémon*: Literacy, new technologies and popular culture in children's everyday lives. In J. Marsh and E. Millard (eds), *Popular Literacies, Childhood and Schooling*. London: Routledge Falmer.

Kress, G. (2003). *Literacy in the New Media Age*. New York: Routledge.

Laidlaw, L. and O'Mara, J. (2011). Living in the iworld: Two literacy researchers reflect on the changing texts and literacy practices of childhood. *English Teaching: Practice and Critique*, 10(4): 149–159. http://files.eric.ed.gov/fulltext/EJ962612.pdf (accessed March 2016).

Livingstone, I. and Hope, A. (2011). Next gen. transforming the UK into the world's leading talent hub for the video games and visual effects industries. *Nesta*. www.nesta.org.uk/sites/ default/files/next_gen_wv.pdf (accessed November 2015).

Marsh, J., Brooks, G., Hughes, J., Ritchie, L., Roberts, S. and Wright, K. (2005). *Digital Beginnings: Young Children's Use of Popular Culture, Media and New Technologies*. Sheffield: Literacy Research Centre, University of Sheffield.

McManis, L. D. and Gunnewig, S .B. (2012). Finding the education in educational technology with early learners. *Young Children*, 67(3): 14–24.

McTavish, M. (2009). I get my facts from the internet: A case study of the teaching and learning of information literacy in in-school and out-of-school contexts. *Journal of Early Childhood Literacy*, 9(1): 3–28.

Ministry of Education (1996). *Te Whāriki, Early Childhood Curriculum*. Wellington: Learning Media.

National Association for the Education of Young Children (2009). *Technology and Young Children*. www.naeyc.org/content/technology-and-young-children/preschoolers-and-kindergartners (accessed October 2015).

National Association for the Education of Young Children and the Fred Rogers Center for Early Learning and Children's Media at Saint Vincent College (2012). *Technology and Interactive Media as Tools in Early Childhood Programs Serving Children from Birth through Age 8*. www. naeyc.org/files/naeyc/file/positions/PS_technology_WEB2.pdf (accessed August 2015).

Neil, C., Brown, C., Sentance, S., Crick, T. and Humphreys, S. (2013). Restart: The resurgence of computer science in UK schools. *ACM Transactions on Computer Education*, 1(1), Article 1, www.twistedsquare.com/CAS2.pdf (accessed September 2014).

New York Daily News (23 April 2013). Hooked on the iPad: Technology addiction affects children as young as 4, experts say. www.nydailynews.com/life-style/health/ipad-addict-4-years-old-article-1.1324900 (accessed October 2015).

Plowman, L., Stephen, C. and McPake, J. (2010). Supporting young children's learning with technology at home and in preschool. *Research Papers in Education*, 25(1): 93–113.

Plowman L., McPake, J. and Stephen, C. (2012). Extending opportunities for learning: The role of digital media in early education. In S. Suggate and E. Reese (eds), *Contemporary Debates in Child Development and Education*. Abingdon: Routledge, pp. 95–104.

Price, H. (n.d.). Homerton Children's Centre, http://ictearlyyears.e2bn.org/resources_71.html (accessed October 2015).

Puerling, B. (n.d.), ASG Education Programmes, NZ. www.asg.co.nz/page.aspx?ID=5435 (accessed October 2015).

School Curriculum Assessment Authority (SCAA). (1996). *Nursery Education: Desirable Outcomes for Children's Learning on Entering Compulsory Education*. London: SCAA and Department for Education and Employment.

Siraj-Blatchford, J., Siraj-Blatchford, I., Pramling, I. and Ramos, J. (2001). *Developmentally Appropriate Technology in Early Childhood* (DATEC) Final Report: A Research and Development Project. www.naeyc.org/files/naeyc/file/positions/PS_technology_WEB2.pdf (accessed August 2015).

STAKES (2004). *National Curriculum Guidelines on Early Childhood Education and Care in Finland*. www.julkari.fi/bitstream/handle/10024/75535/267671cb-0ec0-4039-b97b-7ac6 ce6b9c10.pdf?sequence=1 (accessed October 2015).

Swedish National Agency for Education (2010). *Curriculum for the Preschool, Lpfö 98*. Stockholm: Fritzes.

Tickell, C. (2011). *The Early Years: Foundations for Life, Health and Learning. An Independent Review on the Early Years Foundation Stage*. London: Department for Education.

Yelland, N. (2005). The future is now: A review of the literature on the use of computers in early childhood education (1994–2004). *AACE Journal*, 13(3): 201–232.

Supporting children's technological development

The role of the practitioner

Margrethe Jernes

Introduction

'Take that!', 'Blue – blue – blue!' or 'My turn!' are typical statements in a digital context in kindergarten (Jernes, 2013). Some of the boys are eagerly involved in PC-gaming, and are not aware of one boy waiting for his turn, not getting access. Luckily, a professional practitioner observes and intervenes by effectively organising taking turns and she or he sits down on a small chair close to the children getting involved in the interaction. She puts words to things in the game the children do not understand and she contributes to learning conditions and helps the boys gaming together, not just individually.

The meaningful use of technology in the nursery is completely dependent on knowledgeable professionals who dare to think critically in the situation. This requires broad knowledge about children and relationships as a basis for educational reflection on digital technology. In this chapter, we want to present a pragmatic approach to the use of digital technology in the pre-school. The practitioner's role in a pragmatic sense involves conscious observation to 'capture the moment', the children's zone of proximal development (Vygotsky, 1978: 86) and to act upon this. The aim then is to find the balance.

Technological development through play

Jean Piaget (1896–1980) played a central role in the development of the understanding of the importance of play in children's cognitive development. His theories about learning emphasise the need for children to explore and experiment for themselves, and play appears as an arena for action (Piaget, 1999). For Piaget, play is a means by which children develop and refine concepts before they have the ability to think in the abstract (Bodrova and Leong, 2007: 30). Though there is some dispute over the detail of Piaget's theories, it is now widely accepted that the best way for children to learn is through play; that play is essential and fundamental to a child's physical, social, emotional and intellectual development (Sutton-Smith, 2001).

Research has demonstrated that 'shared activity provides a meaningful social context for learning' (Bodrova and Leong, 2007: 80) and that 'through talking and communicating, the gaps and flaws in one's thinking become explicit and accessible to correction' (ibid.). Vygotsky (1978) suggests that when learning children require activities that both support past learning and encourage new learning at a slightly higher level – activities that are in the zone of proximal development. He also emphasises the importance of imaginative play in child development.

It can therefore be seen that we should ensure that children's technological development is developed through play within a developmentally appropriate environment and that imaginative play should be planned for and encouraged. This chapter will consider that children using technology should engage in collaborative activities in which they are encouraged to talk about their use of technology and their learning, and that practitioners should plan these activities carefully so that they both reinforce prior learning and support new learning.

Practitioners' understanding of children's technological development

It is important that practitioners understand children's technological development and can therefore plan how to support it. When children are introduced to a new piece of technology it is vital that they are given the opportunity and time to explore it for themselves in order, where at all possible, to determine for themselves how it works, how to play with it and learn with it. Children then need to use the technology within different contexts and for different purposes until their understanding of the technology is such that they are able to select that piece of technology appropriately and use it to fulfil a purpose of their own conception (as opposed to fulfilling a purpose that the practitioner has determined). Practitioners must, therefore, proactively encourage the exploration of new technologies and support this process with open-ended questioning so children develop an understanding of not only how the technology works, but also how they can use the technology purposefully, responsibly and safely. Practitioners need to plan activities that involve the use of these developmentally appropriate technologies and develop a learning environment that facilitates and empowers children to make decisions about when it is appropriate to select and use the technologies available to support and enhance their learning.

In this way children will come to use technology as creators; they will begin to use technology as a problem-solving tool; they will be empowered to make choices about their use of technology and to have the confidence to articulate the reasons for those choices. Finally, and very importantly, we hope they will become safe and responsible users of technology.

Background research on digital technology, play and the role of practitioners

Previous research on digital technology in early years has pointed out problem areas associated with the use of technology in children's spontaneous play in kindergarten. It appears that the large weighting of spontaneous play can get the adults to abdicate the arena (Plowman and Stephen, 2006; Plowman *et al.*, 2010), or take a distal approach, as framing the situation rather than being an active part (Plowman and Stephen, 2007). In their significant research with children in a digital world, Plowman and Stephen (2007) found an absence of language when children were using the computer. Also, when the adults were in an activity, the language was poor. In their words:

> When on their own, they rarely initiated talk with other children or adults, either to convey pleasure or to seek help. When using a computer in pairs or groups, as was fairly common, they tended to communicate with each other nonverbally (e.g. taking control of the mouse, moving in closer when they wanted to join in or upending the sand timer used to time sessions when they wanted to prolong their turn) so although there was an appearance of collaborative use of the computer, it was very limited in practice.
>
> (Plowman and Stephen, 2007: 20)

It was striking that the lack of dialogue was typical, even when an adult was part of the interplay. Perhaps the screen itself is taking too much of the focus, and both adults' and children's eyes are being directed to the screen.

Ljung-Djärf's (2008) research revealed that technology was mostly used in spontaneous play where children positioned themselves as either owners, participants or spectators. It was not necessarily cooperation at the computer – the children struggled with positions and positioning (Ljung-Djärf, 2004: 100f). This is validated by Jernes and Engelsen (2012). Studies also point to the importance of pre-school teachers' digital competence (Fischer and Gillespie, 2003) and some give cautions against indiscriminate use of drill and practice programs (Haugland, 2000). Whether technology can provide stimuli to children's learning depends largely on teacher competence (Sheridan and Pramling Samuelsson, 2003; Tsitouridou and Vryzas, 2004). Kindergarten teachers have expressed a desire to strengthen their digital expertise, but they are struggling to find suitable courses and further education, according to an international project across five nations (Saúdea *et al.*, 2004).

The correlation between pre-school teacher and children's digital literacy is also central in other Scandinavian research. Jessen's (2001) action research in educational institutions, where the theme revolved around the creative use of digital tools, raises the issue that creative play is dependent on a knowledgeable child interaction in pre-school. Klerfelt (2007) also discusses the importance of the qualified pre-school teacher. She found that the computer might provide new opportunities to communicate through multimedia possibilities including pictures, words, sound and movement. Digital tools can allow for polyphony where children are given the opportunity to record the spoken language, images can be visualised and the written word may be seen on both screen and paper. This might turn the computer into a story-telling machine, but relies on a cooperative and competent pre-school teacher, as in Lafton's (2012) research.

Barriers and tensions

To increase and develop digital practice in pre-school, the practitioners need both individual knowledge and sufficient equipment. We also know that there are different areas of tension in relation to taking digital technology into practice for pre-school teachers (Jernes et al., 2010). First, within their pedagogical knowledge base, there is a tension between the national curricula and the opportunity practitioners have for making their own choices within their practice. Second, also within pedagogical practice, they are facing the challenges of meeting children's need for exploring digital possibilities and at the same time the need for regulating this. Third, their educational reflections or 'visions' are facing a dilemma. According to Jernes et al. (2010), the practitioners in pre-school seem to concentrate their educational thinking on the applications and techniques, more than on the goals or vision for children's learning. It is, therefore, important to consider how professional practitioners can solve some of the challenges they face in their role of supporting children's digital development.

Supporting technological learning and development

The issue of supporting learning is of fundamental interest in pedagogical thinking. The 'shared activity' is seen as crucial in learning processes (Bodrova and Leong, 2007; Vygotsky, 1978). Research from the EPPE study described sustained shared thinking (SST) as criteria for good-quality learning and development in early years (Siraj-Blatchford, 2009; Sylva et al., 2004). The interaction, characterised as a sustained shared thinking process, is described by the researchers as:

> an episode in which, two or more individuals 'work together' in an intellectual way to solve a problem, clarify a concept, evaluate activities, extend a narrative etc. Both parties must contribute to the thinking and it must develop and extend thinking.
>
> (Sylva et al., 2004: 36)

This philosophy of learning and development is supported by theories from a sociocultural perspective, such as Vygotsky's concept of the *zone of proximal development* where the *more competent other* has an important role (1978: 86). Among others, Bruner et al. (1976) also support the fundamental concept of *scaffolding*.

Mediated learning experience

Communication and dialogue is also described as fundamental in developing thinking (Bakhtin, 2010; Dewey, 1997; Rommetveit, 2003; Vygotsky, 2001). In this light, the philosophy of *mediated learning experiences* (MLE) might contribute to practical pedagogy. Seeing possibilities for strengthening the learning process through mediation, Klein's (1989) theory has its origin in Feuerstein's theoretical approach. Working on mediated learning experiences, the main goal is not working objectively on raising the level of cognitive activity in any area. The goal is rather 'to create flexibility in the child, a desire to learn and the ability to change through new experiences' (Klein, 1989: 27).

The concept *mediating* may, for some of us, be problematic. It can be associated with the paradigm of transferring knowledge within an objectivist view, with the child as an empty vessel to be filled with knowledge (cf. Sommer *et al.*, 2010). In terms of dictionary definitions, it is evident that mediate means to pass on, convey, arrange or impart. However, the concept of mediation can be extended to mean to give, inculcate, announce, assign etc. The main concern, though, is the practitioner's empathic support for cognitive development in a loving and warm interaction. A learn-to-learn process is characterised by an adult who is warm, responsive, non-restrictive and accepting (Klein, 1989). In her research, Klein suggests five criteria for interaction and communication for supporting children's thinking. These are:

1   intentionality and reciprocity;

2   expanding and going beyond the immediate (transcendence);

3   mediating meaning and excitement;

4   mediating feelings of competence; and

5   regulating behaviour by helping the child to plan before acting.

The five principles of working with mediated learning experiences (MLE) in mind might give some guidance for practitioners in situations with children using technology. The first principle concerns the awareness of the purpose and reciprocity. The child and the teacher need to have a mutual understanding of the problem where the intention and focus are common. It might be wanting to write some letters, or searching for their own letter at the computer, for example. The child needs support and guidance along the way in his trial, which means the contact is purposeful and mutual between educator and child.

The second principle is that the educator's ability to pass on meaning and a sense of enthusiasm in the situation is crucial. It may involve conveying our culture, values and norms, respect and wonder. Enthusiasm and communication of feelings may appear as involvement in interactions with children. When the child is searching for his own letters, the practitioner must demonstrate real curiosity for the specific subject, but also connect it to public interest for letters and words, and even for the mysteries of reading and understanding. Maybe the alphabet is on the wall? But this also concerns learning about their own emotional expression and learning to interpret others.

The third principle is the transcendence in the situation. This means an expansion and strengthening of children's experiences and understanding, which relates to the second point in the development pedagogy by Pramling Samuelsson *et al.* (2009). This involves having meta-conversations with the children. The practitioners must be able to go beyond the immediate situation and bring the everyday phenomenon to wondering and scientific thinking. In addition, this way of thinking is inspired by Dewey's (1996) educational philosophy where the hypothesis is central in the 'wondering' and 'doing' experiences. We may use questions such as 'How would it be here at the meal if we did not have chairs to sit on?' or 'How many people in the class do you think have blue eyes?', and then the task is to explore the facts and investigate if the hypothesis was correct or not.

In pre-school the children and practitioners can develop everyday life into effective learning situations, as van Oers (2010) discusses in his article about learning to think, mathematics in play and spontaneous situations. Another example could be wondering together on the difference in thick and thin lines (Figure 6.1) or regular squares against lines that are freely drawn.

The fourth aspect is of great importance for children's development. Practitioners need to be conscious of a communication of acceptance and give the child a sense of mastery. This is in the same spirit as the recognition of 'the other' as a subject (Bae, 2009). It is possible to give the children challenges that we know they can do, but also that they have to work at a bit to manage, in line with Vygotsky's (1978) theory of the zone of proximal development. It might be working on counting the amount of blue eyes in the group, compared to other colours, and filling in a table on the computer. It might be an ordinary worksheet in Excel, or it might be a program developed for children.

The fifth and final element is about regulating behaviour and discussing the coming activity, as activity planning (Klein, 1989: 33f). This might seem quite difficult. When your own theory and pedagogical foundation tell you that children are unique human beings with their own rights and expertise, it might be a challenge to impose regulations, particularly since regulating the behaviour of others may be misunderstood as behaviour modification within behaviourist learning theory. But according to Klein, regulation of the behaviour of others might be done in many

FIGURE 6.1 Using an art program to investigate lines.

ways, for example by the educator as a model in a specific situation. The most central aspect here though is including the child in discussing and talking over what the next step could be in an activity. It might be planning for filling a drawing with colours, planning for drawing his or her family, but it might also be to discuss what the child wants to learn or achieve.

Although the principles are presented separately, they will overlap. However, a certain logical structure in the matter of the first principle must be underlying before the teacher moves onto the next ones. The child and the teacher have to have the same focus in the situation. In a study comparing different teacher approaches when learning with computers, Klein *et al.* (2000) found that mediating adults in the processes of teaching and learning within computer environments had an impact. 'Furthermore,' they say, 'feedback from the teachers who participated in this study indicated that mediational training contributed to the enhancement of their teaching in areas other than those related to the use of computers' (Klein *et al.*, 2000: 604f).

Guided interaction in a digital context

This leads us to the concept of *guided interaction* from Plowman and Stephen's (2007) research. They found that children's confidence and skills in the use of digital tools increases with adult dedication to the same. As mentioned earlier, educators seem to take either a proximal or a distal attitude to playful activity with digital technology. It should be pointed out that the proximal adult in a guided interaction with children can be decisive for good learning outcomes. The distal role is also included in guided interaction, but is more distant and less oriented to face to face. It may be, for example, the purchase of games or the facilitation of the children's activity, i.e. more invisible interaction. Practitioners included in a proximal interaction demonstrate, instruct and organise activities, but also participate in joyful interactions and give positive feedback and support (Plowman and Stephen, 2007: 19). Therefore, the learning environment is characterised by a staff with the necessary technical expertise, both digital and educational. It seems, however, that when kindergartens adopt technology, they are characterised first by equipment and enthusiasm before pedagogical reflection, corresponding to an optimistic technology approach (Jernes *et al.*, 2010).

Reflection on the curriculum: Content, techniques and objectives

In terms of tasks and content in pre-school, the Norwegian curriculum emphasises holistic learning and free play. Digital tools are mentioned once in the second part of the guidance, which give information on everyday play and learning. The guidance states that children in pre-school 'should experience that digital tools can be a source for play, communication and obtaining knowledge' (Ministry of Education and Research, 2011: 27). It does not say that technology *must* or *shall* be used. Compared to a more prescribed curriculum for early years in the UK, this appears very open and gives possibilities for the practitioners' own interpretation of the task. But reflections and interpretation of curricula emerge as a complex area, though necessary for the development of quality in kindergarten. There are several directions in the interpretation of the content of a curriculum. According to Goodlad's (1988) five levels, the curriculum appears on: the ideological (political vision, the idea behind it), the formal (as it physically appears), the perceived (as pre-school teachers interpret it), the implemented (as it came out in practice) and the experienced curriculum (as all participants experienced it). The relationship between educational intentions and practices varies from institution to institution. This is central as grounds for critical reflection on both the curricula and practice (see Chapter 5).

Critical educational reflection includes reflection on content, techniques and the issues of grounds and objectives. Models from the Frankfurter School and critical theory have influenced the development of Klafki's (1998) theory, defined as critical constructive pedagogy. A principle of reciprocity between theory and practice is vital, to avoid a situation in which practice submits to theoretical and prescribed methods/techniques and thereby excludes the need for reflection on practitioners' own educational choices. The term 'constructive' is therefore thinking on the basis of critical analysis of the status quo, constructing new opportunities and encouraging discussion and testing, corresponding to Dewey's (1997) examination activity theory.

Suggestions for practice

Technology with sounds, buttons and colours arouses children's immediate fascination. This can present challenges. It is, of course, beyond all doubt that children should be met as equal fellows in intersubjective relations (Buber, 1996), but pre-school teachers may encounter dilemmas with the satisfaction of immediate needs. The risk is that the children, who get what they want, will not get what they need. Children in kindergarten may prefer to play computer games, but they might benefit more from other physical or creative activities. The challenge then is for the practitioner to find a good balance for the children. Pragmatism is about seeing, assessing and acting wisely (Dewey, 1996), parallel to the notion of 'look, listen and note' in the Early Years Foundation Stage guidance (Siraj-Blatchford, 2009: 6). In practice, this could mean observation and assessment of the interaction that occurs between children and adults when children play for example computer games, draw and write, or do other things with technology, and based on this observation, guiding actions for the benefit of the children. Technological equipment becomes less important here than professional competence in critical educational reflection.

As part of the education process, children can be involved in reflecting and thinking critically about technology (Buckingham, 2007: 150ff), and this ought to be included in the development of digital literacy for both children and adults. Online safety is part of this issue. In working on continuous reflection on everyday practice, we might avoid a focus on narrow technical knowledge or indifferent entertainment. Instead, we should promote critical and independent reflection within our group of practitioners, but also within the group of children. Challenges with technology may be about finding the balance between enthusiasm for new opportunities and assessment of their use as well as outcomes for the children.

When the practitioner focuses first on the children and then on the technology, it appears that activities can be developed into good experiences for the children

(Jernes, 2013). This means to first reflect on the educational goals and vision for children's present and future, and then to consider the technological application and function. This is what can be understood as a pragmatic and balanced approach to technology in early years.

DISCUSSION TOPICS

- What should children know and/or understand about computer systems by the end of the Early Years Foundation Stage?
- How can we develop young children's understanding of safe and responsible use of technology?
- What do the practitioners need in terms of digital knowledge in order to form a reflective judgement of technology for children?

Conclusion

In this chapter we have highlighted some strategies to support children's technological learning and development. One theory put forward is mediating learning experiences (MLE) with children where the practitioner is the key for children's successful outcomes. Another is to understand the practitioner's role in a guided interaction, where the practitioner takes a proximal approach rather than only facilitating technological activities. The third approach we suggest is within pragmatism as philosophy. This involves the practitioner observing the activity, assessing it and then acting wisely upon it, which requires critical educational reflection. Finally, the role of the practitioner in pre-school should be both instructive and mentoring, where a qualified practitioner in supporting children's technological learning and development holds both digital and pedagogical competence.

References

Bae, B. (2009). Children's right to participate – challenges in everyday interactions. *European Early Childhood Education Research Journal*, 17(3): 391–406.

Bakhtin, M. M. (2010). *Speech Genres and Other Late Essays* (Slavic Series, no. 8.). Texas: University of Texas Press.

Bodrova, E. and Leong, D. J. (2007). *Tools of the Mind: The Vygotskian Approach to Early Childhood Education*, 2nd edn. Upper Saddle River, NJ: Pearson Merril Prentice Hall.

Bruner, J. S., Ross, G. and Wood, D. (1976). The role of tutoring in problemsolving. *Journal of Child Psychology and Psychiatry*, 17: 89–100.

Buber, M. (1996). *Jeg og du* [I and Thou]. Oslo: Cappelen.

Buckingham, D. (2007). *Beyond Technology: Children's Learning in the Age of Digital Culture*. Cambridge: Polity.

Dewey, J. (1996). *Erfaring og opdragelse* [Experience and education]. (First published 1938.) København: Christian Ejlers' Forlag.

Dewey, J. (1997). *Democracy and Education: An Introduction to the Philosophy of Education. Første ugave 1916.* New York: Free Press/Simon & Schuster.

Fischer, M. A. and Gillespie, C. W. (2003). One Head Start classroom's experience. Computers and young children's development. *Young Children*, 58(4): 85–91.

Goodlad, J. I. (1988). What some schools and classrooms teach. In J. R. Gress and D. E. Purpel (eds), *Curriculum: An Introduction to the Field*. Berkely, CA: McCutchan.

Haugland, S. W. (2000). Computers and young children. *Clearinghouse on Elementary and Early Childhood Education*, 4(March).

Jernes, M. (2013). *Interaksjoner i digitale kontekster i barnehagen* [Interactions in digital contexts]. Doctoral dissertation (Vol. 186). Stavanger: University of Stavanger.

Jernes, M. and Engelsen, K. S. (2012). Stille kamp om makten. En studie av barns interaksjon i digital kontekst i barnehagen [A quiet struggle for power. A study of children's interaction in a digital context in the kindergarten]. *Nordic Studies in Education*, 32(3–4): 281–296.

Jernes, M., Alvestad, M. and Sinnerud, M. (2010). Er det bra, eller? Pedagogiske spenningsfelt i møte med digitale verktøy i norske barnehager [Is it good? Pedagogical tensions when meeting digital technology in early childhood education]. *Nordisk Barnehageforskning*, 3(3): 115–131.

Jessen, C. (2001). *Børn, leg og computerspil* [Children, play and computer games]. Odense: Odense Universitetsforlag.

Klafki, W. (1998). Characteristics of critical-constructive didaktik. In B. B. Gundem and S. Hopman (eds), *Didaktik and/or Curriculum*. New York: Peter Lang, pp. 307–330.

Klein, P. (1989). *Formidlet læring: om å fremme utvikling i sped- og småbarnsalder* [*Mediated Learning: On encouraging development in infants- and toddlers age*]. Oslo: Universitetsforlaget.

Klein, P., Nir-Gal, O. and Darom, E. (2000). The use of computers in kindergarten, with or without adult mediation; effects on children's cognitive performance and behavior. *Computers in Human Behaviour*, 16, 591–608.

Klerfelt, A. (2007). *Barns multimediala berättande: en länk mellan mediakultur och pedagogisk praktik* [Children's multimedia storytelling: A link between media culture and educational practice]. Doctoral dissertation (Vol. 256). Göteborg: Acta Universitatis Gothoburgensis.

Lafton, T. (2012). How early childhood practitioners build, shape, and construct their digital practices: The search for an analytical space. *Nordic Journal of Digital Literacy*, 7(3): 172–185.

Ljung-Djärf, A. (2004). *Spelet runt datorn: Datoranvändande som meningsskapande praktik i förskola.* [The game around the computer: Computer usage as meaning-making practice in preschool]. Doctoral dissertation (No. 12). Malmö: Malmåo Höskola, Lärarutbildningen.

Ljung-Djärf, A. (2008). The owner, the participant and the spectator: Positions and positioning in peer activity around the computer. *Early Years: An International Journal of Research and Development*, 28(1): 61–72.

Ministry of Education and Research (2011). *Framework Plan for the Content and Tasks of Kindergartens*. Oslo: Norwegian Ministry of Education and Research.

Piaget, J. (1999). *Play, Dreams and Imitation in Childhood*. (First edition 1945.) London: Routledge.

Plowman, L. and Stephen, C. (2006). Technologies and learning in pre-school education. Paper presented at AERA annual meeting, Education Research in the Public Interest, San Francisco, CA.

Plowman, L. and Stephen, C. (2007). Guided interaction in pre-school settings. *Journal of Computer Assisted Learning*, 23: 14–26.

Plowman, L., Stephen, C. and McPake, J. (2010). Supporting young children's learning with technology at home and in preschool. *Research Papers in Education*, 25(1): 93–113.

Pramling Samuelsson, I., Carlsson, M. A., Olsson, B., Pramling, N. and Wallerstedt, C. (2009). The art of teaching children the arts: Music, dance and poetry with children aged 2–8 years old. *International Journal of Early Years Education*, 17(2): 119–135.

Rommetveit, R. (2003). On the role of 'a psychology of the second person' in studies of meaning, language and mind. *Mind, Culture, and Activity: An International Journal*, 10(3): 205–218.

Saúdea, S., Cariocaa, V., Siraj-Blatchford, J., Sheridane, S., Genovd, K. and Nueze, R. (2004). KINDERET: Developing training for early childhood educators in information and communications technology (ICT) in Bulgaria, England, Portugal, Spain and Sweden. *International Journal of Early Years Education*, 13(3): 265–287.

Sheridan, S. and Pramling Samuelsson, I. (2003). Learning through ICT in Swedish early childhood education from a pedagogical perspective of quality. *Childhood Education*, 79: 276–282.

Siraj-Blatchford, I. (2009). Conceptualising progression in the pedagogy of play and sustained shared thinking in early childhood education: A Vygotskian perspective. *Educational and Child Psychology*, 26(2): 77–89.

Sommer, D., Pramling Samuelsson, I. and Hundeide, K. (2010). *Child Perspectives and Children's Perspectives in Theory and Practice*. Dordrecht: Springer.

Sutton-Smith, B. (2001). *The Ambiguity of Play*. Cambridge, MA: Harvard University Press.

Sylva, K., Melhuish, E., Sammons, P., Siraj-Blatchford, I. and Taggart, B. (2004). *The Effective Provision of Pre-School Education (EPPE) Project: Final Report. A Longitudinal Study Funded by the DfES 1997–2004*. London: Institute of Education.

Tsitouridou, M. and Vryzas, K. (2004). The prospect of integrating ICT into the education of young children: The views of Greek early childhood teachers. *European Journal of Teacher Education*, 27(1): 29–45.

van Oers, B. (2010). Emergent mathematical thinking in the context of play. *Educational Studies in Mathematics*, 74: 23–37.

Vygotsky, L. S. (1978). *Mind in Society: The Development of Higher Psychological Processes*. Cambridge, MA: Harvard University Press.

Vygotsky, L. S. (2001). *Tenkning og tale* [Thought and language]. Oslo: Gyldendal Akademisk.

Play in a digital age

Shirley Allen

Introduction

The rapid growth of digital technologies during the twenty-first century has provided young children with access to new contexts for play activities through such devices as electronic game consoles, digital toys, television, computers, smartphones, and iPads or other tablets. This recent upsurge in young children's digital play has been fostered by the increasing portability, affordability and efficiency of digital devices (Flewitt *et al.*, 2015). Additionally, rising numbers of young children have access to the internet and use applications (apps) on their devices (Jones and Park, 2015) (see also Chapter 1).

The use of technology and its potential impact on young children's development

The innovation of young children's engagement in digital play has not occurred without some debate about their use of technology and its potential impact on their development; for instance, concerns about reduced opportunities for children's collaborative free play are aligned with their increased use of 'technologically mediated, consumption-based activities' (Jarvis *et al.*, 2014: 63). It is argued that children's access to screen-based entertainment at home contributes to their inactivity and encroaches on their opportunities to engage in more traditional play experiences, especially within outdoor environments (Brown and Patte, 2013; Tovey, 2007). In a report on the value of children's play, Whitebread *et al.* (2012) noted that some parents and teachers have expressed anxiety about children's use of electronic games that are felt to have violent content or addictive features, though this view was not generally supported by evidence from studies on the subject. According to Stephen and Plowman (2014), concerns about children's use of digital technology can be classified into three main areas of adverse impact: children's health and well-being, their brain development and cognition, and their social and cultural competencies.

At the same time, there are views that suggest a rising level of approval for children's increased engagement in digital play activity (Colwell *et al.*, 2015). Digital technologies are largely perceived by parents as beneficial rather than threatening in nature; they are seen as a useful form of children's entertainment, as well as an educational asset (Lauwaert, 2009). Digital technologies are also thought to present constructive play opportunities, which can promote children's creative, imaginative and social development (Frost, 2010). Some have considered that online and virtual communities extend opportunities for place, time and mode of children's play activity through their access to digital tablets, which have the potential to create new situations within a free play activity (Kalaš, 2010; Wood, 2013, Fleer, 2014). Digital games can also provide a more inclusive platform for children with disabilities than those afforded by real-world games (Byron, 2008). Young children's engagement with digital play is also considered to be beneficial preparation for their adult life; Rosen and Jaruszewicz (2009: 163) suggest that educators and parents appreciate that children 'must learn how to live on a wired planet'.

These perspectives about young children's increased use of digital play prompt further consideration about the role of contemporary play within digital contexts (Edwards, 2014). In focusing on the subject of digital play, this chapter seeks to encourage further exploration of the nature, purpose and value of digital play. However, discussion on digital play first needs to be contextualised within the wider subject of play, so the chapter begins by exploring some theoretical perspectives and practice guidance on young children's play, as these areas influence our understanding of the nature and role of play over time. The chapter then continues to look at notions of play in digital contexts and then considers the role of adults in relation to children's digital play experiences.

Perspectives on play

Play has been categorised into five types, which are commonly described as physical play, play with objects, symbolic play, pretence/socio-dramatic play, and games with rules, which support aspects of children's physical, cognitive and social-emotional development (Whitebread *et al.*, 2012). However, Russell (2013: 171) warns that if play is justified according to its perceived benefits, such as its contribution to children's physical and mental health, then 'it becomes objectified and loses its defining characteristics'. As suggested by Ailwood (2003: 288), 'few authors writing about play would be brave enough to profess to a final definition of play'. This section of the chapter does not seek to provide such a definition of play but aims to explore some perspectives on the subject to support further understanding about the nature of digital play.

'Play is everywhere in Early Childhood Education (ECE)' (Ailwood, 2010: 210). Play is internationally recognised in Article 31 of the United Nations Convention on the Rights of the Child (UNCRC), which affirms the right of the child to engage in age-appropriate play and recreational activities (United Nations, 1989), and is further endorsed within contemporary ECE policy documents as 'integral to effective practice' (Wood, 2010: 11). It is argued, though, that children's right to play is constrained within modern European urban societies due to factors including the effects of contemporary family lifestyles, anxieties about risk and reduced access to play spaces (Whitebread *et al.*, 2012; Brown and Patte, 2013).

As Sutton-Smith (1997) concluded in his seminal study on theoretical perspectives on play, there is much ambiguity about the concept of play. Pedagogical approaches to provision of play in educational settings are also contested; for example, the British Educational Research Association (BERA) Early Years Special Interest Group (2003: 14) queried the efficacy of 'free' play; they noted that 'whilst play forms the bedrock of early learning, an agreed pedagogy of play is less well articulated'. Debates about the nature and efficacy of play are not a recent phenomenon. The benefits of 'free' play were discussed by Plato (c.428–348 BCE), who argued that if children were denied opportunities to play, they would not fully develop as humans. He recommended the creation of 'play sanctuaries', where children could participate in free play (Brown and Patte, 2013).

Natural play

Interest in childhood play emerged during the eighteenth century as a response to progressive urbanisation and industrialisation (Wood, 2014). Rousseau (1712–78) emphasised the value of sensory experiences and playful games in a natural setting. His nostalgic concept of 'natural play' was promoted in Froebel's (1782–1852) child-centred approach to ECE practice; Froebel valued childhood as a stage in its own right and saw play opportunities as a prime pedagogical approach to support children's learning. He introduced the concept of the kindergarten as an educational system for young children which promoted the central importance of play in learning and development. Children had opportunities to explore the natural environment in garden areas of the kindergarten; for instance, Froebel thought play could incorporate brooks and streams that promoted children's experience of building dams, bridges, canals and mills (Frost, 2010). His views on the primacy of play influenced the growth of Forest Schools in Denmark in the 1980s, which promoted play and learning in a natural environment.

Outdoor play

Froebel's views also influenced those working with young children in England at the beginning of the twentieth century, including Margaret McMillan and Susan Isaacs, at a time when rote learning was viewed as the main pedagogical approach to learning. Provision of an outdoor garden area was included in the first 'open-air' nursery for children in 1914 in Deptford, London, which was opened by Margaret McMillan and her sister, Rachel. Children were encouraged to play with natural resources in the nursery garden and had access to tools and movable equipment. However, the garden was largely viewed as a site of compensatory education for disadvantaged children who had poor health conditions rather than as a playful learning environment and recognition of the importance of a garden environment for play-based learning was not sustained at that time (Bilton, 2010).

Provision for garden play was also developed by Susan Isaacs at the Malting House School in Cambridge from 1924–28. Isaacs, who was a trained teacher and psychoanalyst, undertook regular observations of children's play to inform the nursery provision. She viewed the garden as a safe environment where children could express feelings of anger or frustration. Children had access to animals, plants and play equipment and were also offered opportunities for challenge and risk, as Isaacs believed that they could develop skills to be safe and learn responsibility about other living things in their play (Tovey, 2007).

Play and emotional development

The significant role of play in children's emotional development was promoted by Sigmund Freud (1854–1938). From his work as a psychoanalyst, Freud believed play offered a safe context for children to express their emotions. His work was developed further by his youngest daughter, Anna Freud (1895–1982). Both Anna Freud, and her contemporary, Melanie Klein (1882–1960), utilised play in their work to assess childhood trauma and pioneered psychoanalytical approaches to play therapy, which are still widely used with individuals and groups of children who require emotional support. In therapeutic contexts, play can be used as an approach to foster the relationship between the child and practitioner and can support the child to express their feelings and views non-verbally (Adams and Jessiman, 2012).

The importance of interactions between children and their peers or adults in play contexts

Piaget's (1896–1980) work on the importance of children's play activity within a stimulating environment was very influential on ECE during the second part of the twentieth century. Piaget believed that children's knowledge was progressively constructed through their active exploration of an enabling environment. He thought play was primarily an assimilation process; he suggested that during their play children relate new experiences to their existing cognitive schema (Bergen, 2014). However, support of his notion of the child-centred teacher as 'a guide and arranger of the environment, rather than an instructor' (Gray and McBlain, 2012: 61) declined towards the end of the twentieth century with increased interest and understanding of socio-constructivist theories of children's play and learning that emerged in ECE policy and practice at that time.

Vygotsky's (1978) theory on the development of children's play was similar to Piaget's work, though Vygotsky thought that play facilitates children's cognitive, social and emotional, and physical development. He emphasised the importance of the sociocultural context of children's learning and their interaction with adults and more able peers. Vygotsky used the term 'cultural tools' to denote how learning is mediated by tools relating to the child's culture; these could be physical tools, such as the environment, furniture and ways of playing, or psychological tools, such as spoken and written language and notation systems (Jordan, 2010). From his analysis of children's play, Vygotsky thought that play enabled children to operate at a level beyond their development (Gray and MacBlain, 2012). He used the term 'zone of proximal development' (ZPD) to describe a range from what the child could achieve independently at the lower end of the ZPD to what they could achieve with the help and support of others at the higher end of the ZPD (Conkbayir and Pascal, 2014). His work has been highly influential on current ECE policy; for instance, the Early Years Foundation Stage (EYFS) Framework (DfE, 2014) promotes the importance of interactions between children and their peers or adults in play contexts to promote children's learning.

Vygotsky's work was developed by Bruner, who proposed that adults 'scaffold' a task to actively support children's learning; for example, when participating in children's play, the adult might offer a role to the child or model the play (Allen and Gordon, 2011). Rogoff *et al.* (1993) extended Vygotsky's concept of the ZPD with the notion of 'guided participation', which explains how young children acquire meaning from their interactions with others in routine activities. The process of guided participation is described by Rogoff *et al.* (1993: 8) as 'bridging to make connections between the known and the new'; participants in the process 'find a common ground of understanding on which to base their contributions so as to ensure mutual comprehension'. Rogoff *et al.* (1993: 6) also used the term 'cultural tools', which are thought to be 'both inherited and transformed by new members of cultural communities'. The significance of sociocultural contexts was further emphasised by Sutton-Smith (2008: 110), who noted that play should not be simply defined by its representational content; it was also necessary to 'know the cultural context in which the play under consideration takes place in order to evaluate its character'.

Provision for play in early years

Provision for children's engagement in play contexts in ECE settings in the current century has been largely influenced by the findings of the longitudinal Effective Provision of Pre-school Education (EPPE) research project, which proposed that 'excellent settings' offered 'freely chosen yet potentially instructive play activities' (Sylva *et al.*, 2004: 38). This latter view on play is also reflected in the EYFS Framework (DfE, 2014: 9), which advises that 'each area of learning and development must be implemented through planned, purposeful play and through a mix of adult-led and child-initiated activity'. Wood (2013: 48) has challenged the approach to play that is advocated in the EYFS; she considers this terminology 'privileges adults' provision for play' which could be misinterpreted in practice. According to Wood (2013), ECE practitioners are guided by policy statements that refer to play as educationally purposeful but are also exposed to more ideological views on play that encourage them to provide opportunities that support children's 'natural' or 'free' play.

Howard and McInnes (2010) also suggest that terminology used to define play, such as 'adult-initiated', 'child-initiated', 'free-flow', 'structured' or 'unstructured' play can be challenging for practitioners to interpret when implementing a play-based curriculum. Therefore, while provision for play is acknowledged in policy guidance and practice, the practitioner's role of guiding play or enabling children to lead their play is open to different interpretations in practice. Further challenge is provided by prescribed levels of children's outcomes at early stages of their development; practitioners have to balance their assessment of individual children's interests in play against policy guidance on particular age-related 'norms' (Colwell *et al.*, 2015). For example, in their study of playful practice and learning in ECE, McInnes *et al.* (2011) suggested that differences in practitioners' pedagogic interactions with children could be associated with their different perceptions of play and its relationship to children's learning.

The above discussion on perspectives of the form, purpose and value of play demonstrates that the subject draws on 'contrasting disciplinary, theoretical and methodological perspectives' (Wood, 2010: 11). Play can therefore be construed as a complex activity and the practitioner's task of understanding and implementing play can be seen as challenging due to this complexity (Wood, 2013). This has implications for children's play in digital contexts, which is considered next in this chapter.

Implications for children's play in digital contexts

Though the significance of play for young children is widely recognised and much of their use of technology is playful in nature, Marsh (2010) has suggested that the relationship between 'play' and 'technology' is bounded by tensions. Plowman and Stephen (2005: 154), for instance, consider this relationship 'is under-theorised with respect to uses of computers'.

The rapid emergence of digital play contexts for young children offers further ambiguity about the meaning of play, which was discussed previously in the chapter; Sutton-Smith (2008: 116) considered that the dynamic contexts afforded by digital technology have broadened the concept of play as a 'complex phenomenon with many levels'. The chapter now explores the notion of play in digital contexts and considers some implications for practice, which are discussed in the final part of the chapter.

The concept of a toy has changed with the introduction of digital technologies, which have provided additional dimensions to play objects that were previously consigned to a more passive role in their interactions with children in their play (Yelland, 1999). When considering children's opportunities for play in digital environments, Yelland (1999: 217) has called for discussion on the impact of new information technologies '*on* play and *as* play'. In their writing on digital play, Marsh and Hallet (2008: 191) cite Yelland's (1999) view that technology has the potential to not only enhance learning but also promote engagement with ideas in dynamic, new ways; for example, digital toys that enable children 'to engage in fantasy contexts, as well as to create interactions which have personal significance'.

The report 'Digital Beginnings' undertaken by Marsh *et al.* (2005), has helped to inform discussion on the impact of digital technologies on play. Marsh *et al.* (2005) explored the media practices of young children from birth to six years; they found that children were immersed in the use of popular culture, media and new technologies at home and that parents supported their children's interest in these areas through their provision of resources and their interactions with children. The list below details some examples of children's use of technology that were identified from the study; these items particularly relate to digital play, as the focus of this chapter:

- TVs and DVDs, including playing games on TV via the red button;
- computers, for example playing computer games and games on the internet;

- games consoles, for example use of PlayStation®2 EyeToy, which projects children's images on the screen;
- mobile phones, for example playing with toy or discarded phones for 'pretend' conversations or text messaging and for using the camera;
- other technologies, for example using handheld computers to play games, playing with robot pets, playing with electronic toys, such as microwave scanners.

(Adapted from 'Table of activities', Marsh, 2008: 207)

These examples of children's use of technology indicate that they engaged in a range of social and communicative practices, using an array of different online and offline digital play devices. Marsh *et al.* (2005: 77) found that the children, though still participating in non-digital play activities, were 'competent and confident navigators of digital worlds' and concluded that further understanding 'of children's capabilities, needs and potential' in the area of digital activities should be developed.

In a review of research on the subject of digital play, Edwards (2013: 201) noted that the following three main approaches to research have been followed, which involved:

- measuring the extent to which digital play activities can be described as play, when compared to prevailing interpretations of play;
- making comparisons between digital and traditional play activity to see if different types of play are produced;
- taking the play context as a focus to explore if digital play is a response to the cultural location where the technologies are situated and used by children.

The latter approach to research in the above list prompts exploration about how digital play could support the process of children's cultural meaning-making, which was discussed previously in the chapter; this subject has implications for teachers' understanding of how digital technologies might support children's learning or how they might talk critically with children about their digital play (Edwards, 2013).

Children's interaction with digital technologies

The subject of children's interaction with digital technologies has also been investigated by Worthington (2010). From her study of representations that relate to popular culture and digital technologies in children's play, Worthington (2010: 194) suggests that practitioners should focus on children's meaning-making in their play and engage with children in dialogue about the function of their technologies in order 'to scaffold their meanings, enabling them to negotiate and co-construct understandings'. Worthington (2010) advises that children's meanings may not readily be appreciated by adults, especially when little time is available to observe their play; therefore, further analysis of their play is required.

In their report on young children's use of the internet, Holloway *et al.* (2013) noted an increasing trend in young children's access to internet-connected devices and their playful use of virtual world websites, such as Minecraft, Moshi Monsters and Club Penguin. These three-dimensional environments allow children to assume the identity of an avatar and participate in various playful activities, such as games, dressing-up and buying virtual objects to use in their play; they also enable social interaction through players' use of preselected text or their own words (Jones and Park, 2015). It is argued that software programs aimed at children should be open-ended and enable problem-solving activity to encourage them to explore and extend their thinking; conversely, closed programs constrain opportunities for children to make decisions or use their initiative (Johnson and Christie, 2009).

Burke (2013: 59) has described virtual play on websites such as Disney's Club Penguin as 'a new landscape for play and learning' in her study of children's virtual play spaces; she noted that children's lives are influenced by popular culture and driven by a consumer ethos, which impacts on creativity and choices children might make. Concerns have been expressed about children's exposure to commercialised toys that are popularised through digital media, such as toys based on characters from successful films or popular television programmes. However, from her study, Burke (2013: 70) considered that virtual worlds, such as Club Penguin, provide 'immersive spaces where children engage in a plurality of activities and literacies'; for instance, children shared information, engaged in collaborative learning, applied problem-solving skills and could gain respect through their virtual identities from other players on the website. This view is supported by Zevenbergen (2007: 27), who indicated that a sizable number of research studies demonstrate how virtual software and games can extend children's understanding and 'even create new ways of understanding'.

The social context of children's use of digital technologies

When considering the social context of children's use of digital technologies, Lauwaert (2009: 66) noted that prior to the twenty-first century, the geographies of play could be described as a 'one-to-many model', whereby innovation was driven by manufacturers and there was little interaction between the core (company) and 'peripheral users' (consumers). However, since the millennium, much of children's play construction has been facilitated by media and interaction on virtual world play sites. The 'transformation from a one-to-many to a many-to-many geography of play' is described by Lauwaert (2009: 67) as largely coinciding with the change from 'non-digital to digitalized geographies of play'. According to Lauwaert (2009: 67), the many-to-many model has evoked a redistribution of power; it enables easy 'contact and exchange between users' and facilitates companies' participation and access to many-to-many communities.

Offline and online play

From a review of studies on young children's use of virtual world websites, Marsh (2014: 411) argued that it is not possible to distinguish between online and offline domains in contemporary play practices, but suggests that the following three themes occur in digital play:

- Children move fluidly across online and offline domains; genres of offline play (such as socio-dramatic play, fantasy play and games with rules) can be discerned in their play in virtual worlds, just as characters and themes from online virtual world play appear in their offline play contexts.

- Children draw on their experiences and understandings of narratives across different media during their online play.

- Children's ability to manipulate avatars and virtual homes helps them to construct and reconstruct social identities and enables them to take risks and experiment in ways that would not be possible in offline social play.

Electronic/e-books

Young children's use of electronic books, or e-books, provides further opportunities for digital play experiences. E-books, which can be defined as CD-ROM storybooks, or computer, digital or interactive books, might include animations, games, music or sound, which can enhance children's emergent literacy development. The need for adult support is also highlighted when considering children's use of digital texts; according to Barnyak and McNelly (2015) it is important that the book's content and design features are appropriate for the reader in terms of the book's structure, font size and quantity of text per page and that adults support children's use of the book's digital features by modelling and scaffolding their use (see Chapter 3).

Computer programming within digital play contexts

It is also useful to consider young children's experience of programming within digital play contexts. Through using a graphical programming tool on electronic tablets, such as ScratchJr, young children can program their own stories, games, simulations and animations; these devices support children to engage with digital and more traditional concepts of literacy (Kazakoff, 2015). Additionally, simple control interfaces to programmable devices such as the Bee-Bot®, which is a small bee-like robot, enable children to have opportunities to develop the use of increasingly complex directions to move a robot to particular areas or to follow a route (Royal Society, 2012). The following case study is a practitioner's account of their use of programmable toys (Bee-Bots®) with a reception class; this account is followed by a reflective activity.

Case study: Leonie's observations on children's use of a Bee-Bot® in a reception class

We use a programmable toy in our early years setting that is called a Bee-Bot®. It is a bright, colourful programmable floor robot. It enables young children to learn through play about control and directional language. It is easy to use with big arrows and is very robust. It moves accurately in 15cm steps and makes turns of 90 degrees; it also has a large memory of 40 steps. After an initial introduction to the toy, the children in our setting will engage in purposeful exploratory activity, working independently or with peers. Through exploration, the children need to use many different skills; they listen to one another's ideas and develop a shared understanding of how it works. Another advantage of the Bee-Bot® is that no digital recognition is necessary; this enables the children to program the robot by pressing the arrow buttons and then 'go' to make it move. The children enjoy constructing towns for the Bee-Bot® to move around; they then need to give very precise instructions to enable it to move without knocking their models over and need to make predictions before programming. We have always been impressed with how the children from our setting grasp the use of the Bee-Bots®. The only disadvantage for them is that each time the robot completes its instruction, its memory needs to be cleared in order for it to complete its next programme of direction. When not cleared, the Bee-Bot® proceeds by completing the original instruction as well as the new one.

Summary

It is not possible to cover all aspects of play in digital contexts in the space of this chapter; however, some important areas for practice are highlighted in the discussion. These are:

- Children use a range of digital devices and move between online and offline play contexts.
- Play in digital contexts is supported by adults who model use of the technology and can support children's meaning-making in their play.
- Digital technologies are developing in dynamic ways, which prompts the need for further research to promote parents' and practitioners' understanding about children's use of these technologies in their play.

It is also important to consider that children's digital play can subject them to risks and dangers that are associated with internet users; for example, they may experience inappropriate contact or content and commercialism or negative cultural practice, such as cyberbullying (Heider, 2015). However, research to date largely indicates that digital technology has transformed young children's play in a positive way and that its appropriate use can enhance all aspects of their learning (Nutbrown, 2011). In considering dynamic opportunities that might be realised from children's digital play, Kazakoff's (2015) notion of the 'digital divide' should also be considered, whereby children from more advantaged family backgrounds are more likely to engage with digital devices and access the internet at home. The 'digital divide' has implications for children's access to digital play opportunities and the role of the ECE practitioner in supporting young children's use of digital technologies, which is considered further in the final part of this chapter.

Supporting digital play

This chapter concludes by considering support of digital play in terms of its integration into ECE practice and adults' support of children's digital play activities. Though the benefits of young children's access to digital technology are widely recognised, there is evidence of more limited integration of technology in ECE settings (Zevenbergen, 2007; Flewitt et al., 2015). Palaiologou (2014: 6) found that research into young children's use of digital technologies has indicated that young children access technology from an early age at home; however, ECE 'is not yet able to co-participate meaningfully in children's digital experiences'. Additionally, Formby (2014) found that while ECE practitioners accepted the importance of young children's use of technology for their learning, the majority of practitioners used books and non-technology on a daily basis with children. Flewitt et al. (2015: 2) have suggested some factors that may constrain ECE practitioners' use of digital technology. These are:

- the difficulty of integrating digital technology into their literacy planning and practice;
- a curriculum focus on paper-based literacy;
- insufficient time to explore digital resources;
- lack of guidance about the potential of digital technologies;
- low confidence in effective use of digital devices.

Adults' support of children's use of digital technology in their play, and sociocultural theory

It is also important to consider adults' support of children's use of digital technology in their play and sociocultural theory, which was discussed earlier in the chapter. In their study of children's use of computers in pre-school settings in Scotland, Plowman and Stephen (2005) found that though most practitioners used scaffolding in other curriculum areas, it was notably absent within children's play with computers. However, socio-constructivist theories of learning promote the view that 'adults have key roles in creating and sustaining playful learning environments, enabling participation and engagement of all children' (Broadhead et al., 2010: 181). This emphasis on the role of the adult to interact with children during their play activity in order to enhance their learning calls for 'astute and attuned teachers' who can 'capitalize on playful components in learning and learning components in playing' (Johnson, 2014: 189) (see also Chapter 6).

Yelland (2015) has reported on the beneficial effects of adult support of children's use of digital technology in their play, in line with sociocultural theory, as discussed above. From her research on three-year-old children's use of digital video cameras, Yelland (2015) found that, following an initial explanation by their teacher, the children were encouraged to playfully explore their school environment with the cameras.

The teacher then engaged in discussion with the children on their experiences of using the cameras and provided some technical scaffolding on taking photos. According to Yelland (2015), the children became more skilful in operating the cameras and discussed concepts and ideas which arose from their experience of photography, while parents were keen to buy video cameras for their children so they could develop activities initiated by the teacher. In describing this research, Yelland (2015) acknowledges the importance of the teacher's scaffolding of the children's use of the cameras to sustain and develop their playful exploration. Yelland's (2015) example of adult support illustrates how practitioners can extend children's interest in digital technology to enhance their engagement in areas of the ECE curriculum in ways that appear meaningful to children and enable them to 'bring their cultural capital to the classroom' (Nutbrown, 2011: 91).

Digital literacy

The pedagogical approach described above supports a previous call by the Royal Society (RS) (2012) for teaching 'digital literacy'; which is a term used to describe 'how children access, understand and interact with digital technologies' (Palaiologou 2014: 5). Citing Prensky's (2001) term, the 'digital native', the Royal Society (2012: 21) warned that the 'idea that teaching [digital literacy] is unnecessary because of the sheer ubiquity of technology that surrounds young people as they are growing up – the "digital native" – should be treated with great caution'. Stephen and Plowman (2014: 336) have also suggested that children's interaction in digital play via an unfamiliar website or game 'may not come as naturally as the term "digital natives" suggests for children aged three or four'.

ECE practitioners can also model use of digital technology for children in their everyday role in practice. For instance, digital technology provides a useful tool for recording children's play activities and supports the process of partnership working between parents, practitioners and children, as it offers an effective means of sharing children's experiences of playful activities. Digital images of children's play can be used to develop 'Learning Stories', which provide narratives of their play experiences and enable them to revisit and review these experiences, and share them with others (Carr and Lee, 2012).

DISCUSSION TOPICS

■ Consider ways in which young children might experience digital play at home or in early years settings.
  - In what ways do you feel young children's experience of digital play might be beneficial to their learning and development?
  - Do you have any concerns about children's engagement in digital play experiences?
  - Can you match these benefits and/or concerns to any particular digital play activities or contexts?
■ Play in digital contexts.
  - What play experiences do you think are important for young children's learning and development?
  - Which theoretical and/or policy perspectives have informed your understanding of children's play?
  - Are there any aspects of play that you would like to investigate further?
■ Virtual play environments.
  - What is your experience of children's use of virtual play environments?
  - Explore an online virtual play environment and consider how children might benefit from its use.
  - Do you have any concerns about children's use of this or other virtual play environments?
■ Bee-Bot®.
  - From reading Leonie's account of the children's use of a Bee-Bot®, how do you think the children's playful interaction with the Bee-Bot® might extend their play experience?

Conclusion

To conclude, children's use of various digital devices in their play experiences places new demands on ECE practitioners in their daily practice. There are also implications for policy makers and ECE leaders in terms of curriculum guidance and training opportunities for ECE practitioners. As suggested by Stephen and Plowman (2014: 339), it is 'unlikely that children will cease to play with traditional toys in the foreseeable future'. However, if play is considered to be an important medium for learning in ECE, then 'new ways of thinking about play and technology' are required to address this issue 'so that ECE is better equipped to support children's learning' (Edwards, 2013: 201).

Further reading

Ofsted example of good practice in Early Years: Ofsted (2012) *Information and Communication Technology Is Not Just Computers*. www.gov.uk/government/publications/information-and-communication-technology-is-not-just-computers (accessed March 2016).

Edwards, S. (2013). Digital play in the early years: A contextual response to the problem of integrating digital technologies and play-based learning in the early childhood curriculum. *European Early Childhood Education Research Journal*, 21(2), 199–212.

Websites

Tate Kids: Digital play and participation. www.tate.org.uk/context-comment/blogs/tate-kids-digital-play-and-participation

Vitoria and Albert museum: Digital kids. www.vam.ac.uk/content/articles/d/digital-kids/

The CBeebies website provides examples of digital play activities, such as games and jigsaws based on television programme characters: www.bbc.co.uk/cbeebies

References

Adams, R. and Jessiman, L. (2012). Developing through play. In Adams, R. (ed.), *Working with Children and Families: Knowledge and Contexts for Practice*. Basingstoke: Palgrave Macmillan.

Ailwood, J. (2003). Governing early childhood through play. *Contemporary Issues in Early Childhood,* 4(3): 286–299.

Ailwood, J. (2010). Playing with some tensions: Poststructuralism, Foucault, and early childhood education. In Brooker, L. and Edwards, S. (eds), *Engaging Play*. Maidenhead: OUP.

Allen, S. and Gordon, P. (2011). *How Children Learn 4: Thinking on Special Educational Needs and Inclusion*. London: MA Education.

Barnyak, N. and McNelly, T. (2015). Supporting young children's visual literacy through the use of e-books. In Heider, K. and Jalongo, M. R. (eds), *Young Children and Families in the Information Age*. London: Springer.

Bergen, D. (2014). Foundations of play theory. In Brooker, L., Blaise, M. and Edwards, S. (eds), *The Sage Handbook of Play and Learning in Early Childhood*. London: Sage.

Bilton, H. (2010). *Outdoor Learning in the Early Years: Management and Innovation*, 3rd edn. London: Routledge.

British Educational Research Association Early Years Special Interest Group (2003). *Early Years Research: Pedagogy, Curriculum and Adult Roles, Training and Professionalism*. Southwell: BERA.

Broadhead, P., Wood, E. and Howard, J. (2010). Conclusion: Understanding playful learning and playful pedagogies – Towards a new research agenda. In Broadhead, P., Howard, J. and Wood, E. (eds), *Play and Learning in the Early Years*. London: Sage.

Brown, F. and Patte, M. (2013). *Rethinking Children's Play*. London: Bloomsbury.

Burke, A. (2013). Children's construction of identity in virtual play worlds – A classroom perspective. *Language and Literacy*, 15(1): 58–73.

Byron, T. (2008). *Safer Children in a Digital World: The Report of the Byron Review*. Nottingham: DCSF.

Carr, M. and Lee, W. (2012). *Learning Stories: Constructing Learner Identities in Early Education*. London: Sage.

Colwell, J., Beaumont, H., Bradford, H., Canavan, J., Cook, E., Kingston, D., Linklater, H., Lynch, S., McDonald, C., Nutkins, S., Ottewell, S., Randall, C. and Waller, T. (2015). *Reflective Teaching in Early Education*. London: Bloomsbury.

Conkbayir, M. and Pascal, C. (2014). *Early Childhood Theories and Contemporary Issues: An Introduction.* London: Bloomsbury.

DfE (2014). *Statutory Framework for the Early Years Foundation Stage: Setting the Standards for Learning, Development and Care for Children from Birth to Five.* Available at: www.gov.uk/government/publications/early-years-foundation-stage-framework--2 (accessed August 2014).

Edwards, S. (2013). Digital play in the early years: A contextual response to the problem of integrating digital technologies and play-based learning in the early childhood curriculum. *European Early Childhood Education Research Journal,* 21(2), 199–212.

Edwards, S. (2014). Towards contemporary play: Sociocultural theory and the digital-consumerist context. *Journal of Early Childhood Research,* 12(3): 219–233.

Fleer, M. (2014). The demands and motives afforded through digital play in early childhood activity settings. *Learning, Culture and Social Interaction,* 3(3): 202–209.

Flewitt, R., Messer, D. and Kucirkova, N. (2015). New directions for early literacy in a digital age: The iPad. *Journal of Early Childhood Literacy,* 15(3): 289–310.

Formby, S. (2014). *Practitioner Perspectives: Children's Use of Technology in the Early Years.* London: National Literacy Trust.

Frost, J. (2010). *A History of Children's Play and Play Environments.* London: Routledge.

Gray, C. and MacBlain, S. (2012). *Learning Theories in Childhood.* London: Sage.

Heider, K. (2015). Cybersafety in early childhood: What parents and educators need to know. In Heider, K. and Jalongo, M. R. (eds), *Young Children and Families in the Information Age.* London: Springer.

Holloway, D., Green, L. and Livingstone, S. (2013). *Zero to Eight. Young Children and Their Internet Use.* London: EU Kids Online. http://eprints.lse.ac.uk/52630/1/Zero_to_eight.pdf (accessed July 2015).

Howard, J, and McInnes, K. (2010). Thinking through the challenge of a play-based curriculum. In Moyles, J. (ed.) *Thinking about Play: Developing a Reflective Approach.* Maidenhead: OUP.

Jarvis, P., Newman, S. and Swiniarski, L. (2014). On 'becoming social': The importance of collaborative free play in childhood. *International Journal of Play,* 3(1): 53–68.

Johnson, J. (2014). Play provisions and pedagogy in curricular approaches. In Brooker, L., Blaise, M. and Edwards, S. (eds), *The Sage Handbook of Play and Learning in Early Childhood.* London: Sage.

Johnson, J. and Christie, J. (2009). Play and digital media. *Computers in the Schools: Interdisciplinary Journal of Practice, Theory, and Applied Research,* 26(4): 284–289.

Jones, I. and Park, Y. (2015). Virtual worlds: Young children using the internet. In Heider, K. and Jalongo, M. R. (eds), *Young Children and Families in the Information Age.* London: Springer.

Jordan, B. (2010). Co-constructing knowledge: Children, teachers and families engaging in a science-rich curriculum. In Brooker, L. and Edwards, S. (eds), *Engaging Play.* Maidenhead: OUP.

Kalaš, I. (2010). *Recognizing the potential of ICT in Early Childhood Education.* Moscow: UNESCO Institute for Information Technologies in Education.

Kazakoff, E. (2015). Technology-based Literacies for Young Children: Digital Literacy through Learning to Code. In Heider, K. and Jalongo, M. R. (eds), *Young Children and Families in the Information Age.* London: Springer.

Lauwaert, M. (2009). *The Place of Play: Toys and Digital Cultures.* Amsterdam: Amsterdam University Press.

Marsh, J. (2008). Media literacy in the Early Years. In Marsh, J. and Hallet, E., *Desirable Literacies: Approaches to Language and Literacy in the Early Years,* 2nd edn. London: Sage.

Marsh, J. (2010). Young children's play in online virtual worlds. *Journal of Early Childhood Research,* 8(23): 23–39.

Marsh, J. (2014). Media, popular culture and play. In Brooker, L., Blaise, M. and Edwards, S. (eds), *The Sage Handbook of Play and Learning in Early Childhood.* London: Sage.

Marsh, J. and Hallet, E. (2008). *Desirable Literacies: Approaches to Language and Literacy in the Early Years*. London: Sage.

Marsh, J., Brooks, G., Hughes, J., Ritchie, L., Roberts, S. and Wright, K. (2005). *Digital Beginnings: Young Children's Use of Popular Culture, Media and New Technologies*. Sheffield: Sheffield University.

McInnes, K., Howard, J., Miles, G. and Crowley, K. (2011). Differences in practitioners' understanding of play and how this influences pedagogy and children's perceptions of play. *Early Years: An International Research Journal*, 31(2): 121–133.

Nutbrown, C. (2011). *Key Concepts in Early Childhood Education and Care*, 2nd edn. London: Sage.

Palaiologou, I. (2014). Children under five and digital technologies: Implications for early years pedagogy. *European Early Childhood Education Research Journal*. DOI: 10.1080/1350293X.2014.929876.

Plowman, L. and Stephen, C. (2005). Children, play, and computers in pre-school education. *British Journal of Educational Technology*, 36(2): 145–157.

Prensky, M. (2001). Digital natives, digital immigrants. *On the Horizon*, 9(5): 1–6.

Rogoff, B., Mistry, J., Goncu, A. and Mosier, C. (eds) (1993). Guided participation in cultural activity by toddlers and caregivers. *Monographs of the Society for Research in Child Development*, 58(8) Serial No. 236.

Rosen, D. and Jaruszewicz, C. (2009). Developmentally appropriate technology use and early childhood teacher education. *Journal of Early Childhood Teacher Education*, 30(2): 162–171.

Royal Society (2012). *Shut Down or Restart? The Way Forward for Computing in UK Schools*. London: The Royal Society.

Russell, W. (2013). Towards a spatial theory of playwork: What can Lefebvre offer as a response to playwork's inherent contradictions? In Ryall, E., Russell, W. and Maclean, M. (eds), *The Philosophy of Play*. London: Routledge.

Stephen, C. and Plowman, L. (2014). Digital play. In Brooker, L., Blaise, M. and Edwards, S. (eds), *The Sage Handbook of Play and Learning in Early Childhood*. London: Sage.

Sutton-Smith, B. (1997). *The Ambiguity of Play*. Cambridge, MA: Harvard University Press.

Sutton-Smith, B. (2008). Play theory: A personal journey and new thoughts. *American Journal of Play*, 1(1): 80–123.

Sylva, K., Melhuish, E., Sammons, P., Siraj-Blatchford, I. and Taggart, B. (2004). *The Effective Provision of Pre-School Education [EPPE] Project: Final Report*. Nottingham: DfES.

Tovey, H. (2007). *Playing Outdoors: Spaces and Places, Risk and Challenge*. Maidenhead: OUP.

United Nations (1989). *Convention on the Rights of the Child*. New York: United Nations.

Vygotsky, L. (1978). *Mind in Society: The Development of Higher Psychological Processes*. Cambridge, MA: Harvard University Press.

Whitebread, D. with Basilio, M., Kuvalja, M. and Verma, M. (2012). *The Importance of Play: A Report on the Value of Children's Play with a Series of Policy Recommendations*. Brussels: Toy Industries of Europe.

Wood, E. (2010). Developing integrated pedagogical approaches to play and learning. In Broadhead, P., Howard, J. and Wood, E. (eds), *Play and Learning in the Early Years*. London: Sage.

Wood, E. (2013). *Play, Learning and the Early Childhood Curriculum*, 3rd edn. London: Sage.

Wood, E. (2014). The play-pedagogy interface in contemporary debates. In Brooker, L., Blaise, M. and Edwards, S. (eds), *The Sage Handbook of Play and Learning in Early Childhood*. London: Sage.

Worthington, M. (2010). This is a *different* calculator – with computer games on: Reflecting on children's symbolic play in the digital age. In Moyles, J. (ed.), *Thinking about Play: Developing a Reflective Approach*. Maidenhead: OUP.

Yelland, N. (1999). Technology as play. *Early Childhood Education Journal*, 26(4): 217–220.

Yelland, N. (2015). Young children as multimodal learners in the information age. In Heider, K. and Jalongo, M. R. (eds), *Young Children and Families in the Information Age*. London: Springer.

Zevenbergen, R. (2007). Digital natives come to preschool: Implications for early childhood practice. *Contemporary Issues in Early Childhood*, 8(1): 19–29.

8

Creativity in a digital age

Beverley Barnaby and Victoria Burghardt

Introduction

In a world where young children are increasingly exposed to and engaged with a wide range of digital technologies, it is important to consider the potential implications for child development and education. In this chapter, benefits and risks will be assessed with regard to young children's creativity when using this type of media. In doing so, the pedagogies and practices that are likely to enhance the use of technology for creative thinking will be considered. These pedagogies and practices are based on 'principles' taken from the UK Statutory Framework for the Early Years Foundation Stage (EYFS) (DfE, 2014). This includes consideration of 'Enabling Environments', 'Positive Relationships' and respect for the 'Unique Child'. The chapter will consider how these principles may be applied to nurturing creativity with the use of information technology. It will be argued that it is not the mere presence of technological resources which permit a child to think creatively; it is the way the technology is used.

Creativity and technology

Information technology (IT) incorporates the use of equipment which can store, retrieve, transmit and manipulate data. This may include screen-based media such as computers or tablets, and other equipment such as whiteboards, digital cameras and recorders. The capabilities and applications of such equipment are becoming ever more flexible; smartphones and tablets, for example, both incorporate cameras. Digital data can take the form of letters, numbers, or symbols that refer to, or represent, conditions, ideas or objects. The resulting text, graphics, audio and visual information are collectively termed 'digital media' (Daintith, 2009).

Experts continue to debate the precise definition of creativity, although there is some consensus as to contributing characteristics: divergent thinking, innovation, original and flexible thought, and exploration of ideas. Sternberg (2003) suggests that creative thinking is imaginative, original and produces ideas of value.

The relationship between imagination and creativity is not straightforward. Although it is undeniable that young children can be imaginative, it is debatable as to whether they are able to produce original knowledge, or ideas that are of value. However, their creative output may be original and hold value, at least to themselves.

Although creativity is often primarily associated with activities such as painting, crafts, music or drama, it can be considered within a wide range of other activities related to areas of learning across the early years curriculum.

Young children's relationship with technology in a digital world

When focusing on the role of digital media in children's creative development, we need to question not only childcare pedagogies and practices in the early years, but also the role that technologies play more generally in a child's life.

At home a child will be exposed to technology in every room of their house; for example, the kitchen may be filled with electronic gadgets from microwave ovens to digital weighing scales. Children will see parents and older siblings using IT: internet activity, researching, reading, creating, and playing games using computers, tablets, smartphones, MP3 players and cameras. Children, as with other family members, are likely to watch TV, download films, and listen to recorded music. Even very young children are quite likely to own an array of technology: interactive toys, laser games, moving characters and speaking books (Rideout et al., 2003) (see also Chapter 1).

Albert Bandura (1977) suggests that children learn by imitating role models. It is, therefore, not surprising that very young children will want to copy their parents and siblings who are using technology (Lauricellaa et al., 2015). If children see others using technology and digital media for creative pursuits (such as audio-visual production), it follows that they will be more likely to attempt to employ technology in a creative way (see Chapter 2).

The increasing significance of screen-based media on young children's lives has generated concern among some parents, early years educators and academics (Christakis et al., 2004). The amount of time children spend with computers, tablets and smartphones may need to be balanced with more active, social and creative pursuits, all seen as important contributing factors for development and well-being.

Personal computers can be perceived as presenting a more restrictive learning environment than the 'real world'. As children tend to use screen-based media indoors and in a sedentary way, their relationship with technology could lead to a reduction in more physical, outdoor activities known to facilitate development, including creative thinking.

Tablets and smartphones are also potentially addictive, and may displace children's natural urge to play and create. There is some empirical evidence regarding the addictive nature of screen-based media (Moeller, 2011), and a solitary and passive screen-based culture may contribute to developmental delay in children (Palmer, 2007). Parents and practitioners, therefore, have an important role to play in supervising the time spent on activities, to ensure that there is a balance of play experiences encountered by the child.

Creativity, digital media and the Early Years Foundation Stage Framework

Practitioners in early years settings in the UK are required by law to follow the Early Years Foundation Stage Curriculum (EYFS) (2014). Within this framework, there are several opportunities for children to nurture their creativity within the seven areas of learning and development outlined. The more obvious areas for using digital media in a creative way include 'Expressive Arts and Design', in which children should be encouraged to explore and play with a wide range of media and materials, through a variety of activities in art, music, movement, dance, role play, and design and technology (DfE, 2014).

Within the Early Learning Goals for Expressive Arts and Design, children are expected to experiment with, and create their own ideas, using different materials, tools, instruments, and digital media, by exploring, for example, colour, texture, music, dance, stories and role play. In another of the seven areas of learning and development, 'Understanding the World' (and corresponding learning goal, 'Technology'), children are expected to recognise that a range of technology is used in places such as homes and schools. They are also expected to be able to select and use technology for particular purposes. For example, children may use technology to explore within the following themes: finding out, images and light, toys and machines, making marks and exploring sounds (Hertfordshire ICT Scheme, 2012–2013).

Although the learning areas mentioned explicitly describe potential opportunities for developing creativity through technology, digital creativity can be employed in the other prescribed areas of learning: Communication and Language; Physical Development; Personal, Social and Emotional Development; Literacy; Mathematics.

Technology may be able to enhance learning, creative thinking and creative output, but it is unlikely, in itself, to transform poor teaching and learning into 'good' or 'creative' experiences. This will only come from integrating digital media with the best early years pedagogies.

The EYFS (2014) suggests that children generally learn best through 'actively playing and exploring, by children investigating and experiencing things, and "having a go"'. It suggests that children learn most effectively when they are thinking creatively and critically to make links between ideas, and to develop their own ideas (DfE, 2014).

Constructivist and stage theorists, such as Jean Piaget, Jerome Bruner and Lev Vygotsky have outlined the thought processes of young children which underpin the developmental stages and processes, which can be related to creative thinking. The work of these theorists, and of early years pioneers such as Friedrich Froebel (1782–1852) and Maria Montessori (1870–1952), has continued to inform early years practice in the UK. When implemented effectively, these pedagogies provide opportunities to nurture creative thinking, enhancing children's cognitive development and social and emotional well-being.

It is expected that settings will support the development and learning of young children. The guiding principles of the EYFS require that early years practitioners respect a child's uniqueness, and foster their natural ability to learn and create. Children require an enabling environment and positive relationships between themselves, their family, practitioners and other children, in order to develop their abilities, confidence and independence.

Nurturing environments

Froebel and Montessori considered freedom and choice to be fundamental to learning through play. The educationalist John Dewey (1859–1952) also suggested that children learn best when they have the freedom to explore their environment, with the opportunity for learning through 'hands-on' experience. He suggested that this allows children to build on their natural instincts to investigate, to express themselves and to be creative (Dewey, 1938).

Piaget saw children as natural 'little scientists'. They are born ready to engage and learn from their world, by using their senses and movements to 'experiment' with objects and ideas. He believed that learning about the world is a constructive *and* creative process, in that children are continually 'assimilating' and 'accommodating' information to shape their 'schema' (Piaget, 1952). He, therefore, believed that children placed in a stimulating environment with a range of open-ended opportunities would develop deep learning, and the ability to think critically and creatively through exploration and experimentation (ibid.).

Piaget proposed that children's cognitive development occurs in stages, due to the development of their 'schema'. It follows, therefore, that children should have access to resources and opportunities which are developmentally appropriate.

In the first eighteen months, young children are mainly developing cognitively through senses, fine and gross motor activity. Piaget described this as the 'sensorimotor stage' (ibid.). As children's thinking is not yet flexible enough to link and combine ideas to produce identifiable original ideas, they are not seen as capable of thinking creatively. However, they can still be introduced to digital and creative resources to prepare them for more creative play in subsequent years. Younger children can be introduced to the functioning of equipment by using toys, and replicas of digital equipment, for example toy mobile phones and cameras. Adults can provide stimulation by introducing young children to digitally produced images and sounds, for example, videos, and books with multimedia features, which have been found to have some positive effect on expressive vocabulary (Takacs *et al.*, 2015).

From eighteen months to five years, as children's language develops, Piaget felt that children begin to engage in *symbolic* and make-believe play. He termed this period of development as the pre-operational stage (Piaget, 1952). During this stage, toddlers should therefore be able to use replica technology and digital toys in self-directed, self-created, role-play activities. They can also be guided in the use of simple screen-based media, permitting symbolic play through the use of drawing packages and programmable toys. Developing motor skills and cognitive abilities will permit older children to use an increasing range of IT and digital media within their play. The increased flexibility of their thought processes will allow them to make more original links between ideas, digital media and non-digital resources, increasing their ability to develop creative thinking.

If early years settings intend to build upon children's familiar experiences they need to include digital media alongside more traditional resources. Creating new ideas also requires space and time, with the opportunity to make links across physical environments, with a variety of materials and media, using different sensory modalities. The flexibility of space, time and resources encourages flexibility of thought (Cremin *et al.*, 2006).

Within an early years setting, therefore, it is advantageous to have 'free-flow' discovery play to encourage creative thinking. Tina Bruce explains 'free-flow play' as play which is freely chosen and child-led. It requires an open-plan layout, including a variety of play areas and materials within indoor and outdoor environments. These allow children to freely rehearse activities and to use their imagination. Free-flow play allows children to immerse themselves fully, or to 'wallow' in self-directed activity (Bruce, 2011). Total immersion in activities has been identified as a precursor to, and effect of, creative learning (Csikszentmihalyi, 1996).

As creative thinking requires flexible space and time, it makes sense to have a range of IT and other digital media as freely available as other traditional creative play media. It also requires children to have free *time* to access the equipment and media. However, this does not mean that early years environments need to be a disorganised 'free for all'. In an early years setting, there may be areas designated for different types of purposeful play, for example, dressing-up play, muddy play, messy play, arts and crafts, reading, music, and televisual equipment.

Screen-based media may be seen as presenting a more restrictive learning environment, contradictory to 'free-flow' play and creative thinking. However, computers can potentially provide a 'free-flow, virtual environment', offering many opportunities for children to be creative. Different computer applications allow children to mix data, and to link ideas in original ways, encouraging them to be creative. Children can be taught to transport ideas from one application to another, enabling them to experiment and explore in an open-ended fashion. Mobile computing devices such as tablets, smartphones and digital recording devices can be easily incorporated into free-flow play activities.

Free-flow play may be interspersed with more controlled, structured sessions, with some limits placed on the number of children using particular equipment. This has benefits with regards to organising and protecting equipment, and to issues of health and safety. If a child paints the computer screen, it may show a creative spirit but could result in an expensive and dangerous outcome!

Positive relationships

Although the 'freedom' to explore their environment can encourage children's creative thinking, positive relationships can also enhance the learning experience. Children learn not only through experimentation, but by having new ideas put to them, new skills taught and modelled to them, and being supported in their thinking by others.

Vygotsky (1978) maintained that children learn best when they are suitably challenged and appropriately guided by a 'more knowledgeable other'. He believed that the adults should recognise the child's current level of thinking, in order to set an achievable but challenging goal to help them to another level. This is encompassed within the EYFS: 'Practitioners must respond to each child's emerging needs and interests, guiding their development through warm, positive interaction' (DfE, 2014). This is as true in developing creative thinking as it is in nurturing other developmental areas. Bruner describes the effective support and guidance given to children as 'scaffolding' (Bruner in Wood *et al.*, 1976). Whether a child is engaged in a structured task organised by a practitioner, or in a child-led creative activity, the adult may still identify the opportunity to encourage further learning in any situation.

An idea might be generated by an adult, resulting in a creative activity based around the child's own ideas and preferences. If a child is not sure how to progress, an adult is there to model and support the use of the technology, and to guide the child with questions like, 'What if…?' and 'What else is possible?', which are found to develop creative thinking (Cremin *et al.*, 2006). The adult may also see a potential of the digital media that the child has not seen, which could deepen their learning and creative thinking. Hargreaves *et al.* (2003) in Alexander (2008), argued that active involvement alone is not sufficient to lead to deep learning. They believe that 'dialogic teaching' (which requires talk to engage and extend thinking) is needed. This requires an environment where children feel free to take risks and share ideas to solve problems related to educational goals (Alexander, 2008).

Apart from one-to-one teaching and guidance, another role of the adult in an early years setting is to encourage collaboration between children. This is not only to help the child to develop social and language skills, but to share and evaluate their knowledge, thereby enhancing their cognitive development. Play and collaboration have been found to be key motivators to creative thinking (Sawyer, 2008).

Children naturally move from playing in 'parallel' to 'co-operative play' (Parten, 1932). As children get older they begin to talk to each other about their play and to combine their shared ideas to create new ones. The role of the adult is then to encourage interaction in order to stimulate potential creative thinking. IT and digital media can facilitate this process. Children can work together to operate and apply technology. They may use it to create scenarios within their role play, using devices such as mobile phones, digital scales and keyboards. They may use karaoke machines and recording machines to create music together, or the whiteboard to stimulate the creation of a new dance routine. Also, children can use digital cameras and videos to capture aspects of their daily play without interruption, giving them the freedom to think creatively in deciding what to record.

A unique child

In practice, young children's creative thinking is assessed through their language and play behaviour. Early years educators look at how children develop their own ideas, make links between ideas, and the processes they use to develop creative strategies. These characteristics are identified in the EYFS (DfE, 2014) and are readily observed in children during a range of pursuits, which go beyond the usual understanding of 'creative' activities. As Meadows (2004: 142) noted, 'We do not directly observe thinking or other cognitive processes, we infer them from observable behaviour.' If chidlren are given a stimulating environment, and adult support and encouragement (enhanced by digital media), then they are likely to be seen using their imagination, developing their own ideas, making links between ideas, and developing strategies.

Assessing children formatively is integral to their development and learning. It involves practitioners observing children to understand their progress and interests, and to then plan for the next steps.

Creative thinking will often arise when a child is engaged in an activity, so it is important for the practitioner to have knowledge of the child's preferences. Children may have preferences for particular types of creative pursuits: visual, construction, music, story-telling, number/science, or role play. Creative thinking can be encouraged in any of these, and potentially enhanced with technology and digital media.

> Practitioners must consider the individual needs, interests, and stage of development of each child in their care, and must use this information to plan a challenging and enjoyable experience for each child in all of the areas of learning and development.
>
> (DfE, 2014)

Digital technology can make it easier to assess children's creative thinking processes through recordings of their creative activity. These digital products may be of value to adults, parents and other children for further learning/teaching and assessment opportunities.

Settings must have arrangements in place to identify any children who need additional support. Given the necessary support, creative experiences can be accessed by all children through the use of digital media. Due to the range of ways that children can connect with technology, it provides almost instant access to differentiated, creative opportunities. Differentiation by resource, activity and grouping can help to meet children's individual needs, including in terms of developing creative thinking (Medwell, 2007). Technology can increase the likelihood of creative achievement through personalised learning, thereby enhancing experiences, particularly for children with SEN (Organisation of Economic Cooperation and Development, 2001).

Digital media for creative practice

Screen-based media

Screen-based media and other digital devices should be viewed as 'tools' for creating. Some research suggests that teachers of early years education are yet to discover the full potential for the use of technology as a tool for creative learning (Morgan, 2010). Computers, tablets and smartphones offer children access to imaginary worlds that allow them to create in ways that they could not do naturally. This can then enable young children to become lost in open-ended and magical journeys. Depictions of people and animals from around the world can be displayed on computers and whiteboards, immediately expanding the boundaries of the early years setting. Digital media may provide access to a limitless supply of stimuli for inspiring and initiating creative thinking: ideas for pattern-making, art, crafts, construction, story-telling, music and games.

Role play encourages creative thinking; digital media such as television and videos can be used to stimulate this type of creative play. For example, children will watch popular children's characters from TV and video, which inspire them to take on roles, and create their own way of acting out stories. Children's television may also stimulate creative activity by demonstrating how to make interesting items to be developed further by children's own imagination. For example, an episode of a children's arts and crafts programme might demonstrate how to make a cake from sponges and paper. A child may copy and elaborate on the design, before using the cake in their role play.

There are a multitude of applications (apps) available for young children which can be used to generate creative outputs. For example, some apps encourage children to speak or sing to the animated character, which then echoes the child's creation, encouraging further creative involvement. Others encourage children to combine colours and shapes to create their own designs.

Drawing and design packages are also readily available to use on personal computers and tablets. However, in order to stimulate creative thinking, a child may need to be shown the potential for it to be combined with other virtual and real-world media. If we use technology to try to encourage creativity in children, for example teaching a child to create art using screen-based 'paint' software to make a greetings card, then it is important to ensure that it is an effective teaching method and part of a genuinely creative process. To create a card, a child may take a photograph using a digital camera, upload the photograph onto a computer, print it off, and add their own embellishments using paint and collage. Open-ended tasks not only produce a range of outcomes, but allow for self-expression, with respect to the unique interests of the child.

It could be argued that a child who is shown how to construct a greetings card as modelled by a practitioner will potentially develop a number of physical, cognitive, language and social skills. However, the extent to which it would nurture creative thought is debatable, as the card is unlikely to be 'original' in its design. However, if it is suggested by a practitioner that a child makes a card using any medium, including digital media, then the output could be more original, and may entail more creative thinking. Therefore, whether digital devices and information technology can be used as effectively as traditional non-digital devices for nurturing creativity will depend on the child's interests, the environment, and the adults' contributions. If the child views IT as a tool which can help to integrate ideas and media, then its power to aid creative thinking and creative outputs can be more fully explored.

Mixing 'real' and virtual media

Mobile computing devices such as tablets and digital recording devices have made it easier for a child to cross spatial boundaries, allowing the flexibility to mix media, using cross modalities (mixing sights and sounds). Words, pictures and sounds can be woven together, supporting children to express their ideas, thoughts and feelings creatively. For example, children may listen to a story, and then try and retell different parts of the story using a digital recorder. Children could illustrate their story using paints or software (or a mixture of the two) and the resulting illustrations can be scanned into the computer. Children could use digital and non-digital items from around the nursery to produce sound effects related to the story. The adult may demonstrate how the story, sounds and pictures can be integrated to produce a final digitally displayed product. The activities will undoubtedly encourage imagination, creative thinking and nurture a multitude of other skills. The technology will have facilitated a collaborative, inclusive, multimodal original presentation.

Mathematics and science may not seem such an obvious target for creative media. However, software can encourage children to think about maths in creative ways by integrating number into stories and games. Children could participate in a cookery invention activity, measuring out ingredients using a digital weighing machine. Outdoors they could use a see-saw to explore balance using a variety of random items. These activities can be recorded, displayed on a whiteboard and further evaluated by the children and practitioners. Many early years educators see digital media as a way to support creativity, not to displace it.

It is widely accepted that creativity requires the freedom to take risks and to make 'mistakes', often challenging conformity and boundaries, physical, social and emotional (Burnard *et al.*, 2006). Therefore, there may be greater risk involved when children are allowed to be creative with technology. Breakages are inevitable and setting insurance would be invaluable.

Risk and safety

Children entering an early years setting need to learn the norms and rules of the setting. However, a 'too formal', rule-bound environment can restrict learning in general, and more specifically in terms of creative thinking. Piaget felt that the best learning was child-led. However, child-led learning should not be confused with letting the child 'get on with it'.

Early years practitioners, therefore, need to balance a culture of 'choice' with the need to keep children safe from harm (DfE, 2014). There have to be rules about the safe and effective use and storage of technological equipment. Internet use can be initiated by the practitioner or child, although access to the internet always needs to be properly secured and monitored (see Chapter 9). Screen-based media often relies on young children touching and sliding their small index finger across the screen. According to the British Educational Communications and Technology Agency (2001), there are concerns that too much physical interaction, using fingers, may cause repetitive strain injuries, therefore the time spent using such media needs to be considered. If digital media are used in a safe and developmentally appropriate manner, they can stimulate and strengthen play experiences and encourage young children to express themselves in a creative way. Practitioners will have to decide when a child is sufficiently prepared to use different digital equipment, just as they would other types of indoor and outdoor equipment.

There may be a temptation for adults to leave children to play as long as they are happily engaged and not being disruptive. Children often find both creative pursuits and technology absorbing, and it is in this immersed state that some of the best learning can occur. For example, some educational computer games have the potential to immerse children in a virtual world of problem-solving, requiring them to think critically and creatively. However, technology can be absorbing without nurturing deep learning; watching the television absent-mindedly and playing 'quick reward' computer games are examples. If children are left playing on a computer for long periods of time, there is a risk that learning could become repetitive and shallow. Adult guidance is needed to ensure that the child is benefitting from their experiences by extending their knowledge, and encouraging the child to think creatively.

FIGURE 8.1 Example of how a four-year-old has taken a digital photograph of herself, transferred it to a paint program on a tablet, and is decorating the picture.

DISCUSSION TOPICS

- What is your understanding of 'digital creativity'?
- Consider some practical examples of the ways in which technology can enhance and develop young children's creativity.

Conclusion

Having discussed the role that digital media plays in promoting children's creativity, through examining the guiding themes of the Early Years Foundation Stage (2014), good childcare practices and pedagogies, and potential risks to their development, it is evident that this type of media offers many different opportunities for children to develop creatively. Children, using digital media, need to be given access to experiences that allow them to explore and link ideas, think in novel and open-ended ways and gain access to an imaginary world. In order to understand the process of such activities, it may be important to focus on the concept of 'digital creativity' whereby digital technology and creative thinking are seen as more interrelated and less polarised.

As young children are growing up in a world in which they are increasingly exposed to and engaged with a wide range of digital technologies, it is important to be mindful that their natural ability and propensity to create is being promoted and not suppressed by this medium. Whereas over-use of digital media (whereby young children are left unsupervised for long periods of time), and using media that is not developmentally appropriate, may be detrimental to children's development, a more adult-facilitated approach can serve to nurture young children's creative thinking. The success of developing creativity in the early years through the use of digital media is reliant upon a targeted selection of 'tools' allied to appropriate pedagogical approaches taken by teachers (Webb and Cox, 2004). The relationship that children in the early years have with this media can empower them to make choices and create their own ideas – the main characteristics of effective learning (DfE, 2014).

References

Alexander, R. (2008). *Dialogic Teaching*, 4th edn. York: Dialogos.

Bandura, A. (1977). *Social Learning Theory*. Englewood Cliffs, NJ: Prentice-Hall.

British Educational Communications and Technology Agency (2001). *Keyboard Skills in Schools*. Coventry: BECTA. www.becta.org.uk/technology/infosheets/index (accessed November 2014).

Bruce, T. (2011). *Cultivating Creativity: For Babies, Toddlers and Young Children*, 2nd edn. London: Hodder Education.

Burnard, P., Craft, A. and Grainger, T. (2006). Possibility thinking. *International Journal of Early Years Education*, 14(3): 243–262.

Christakis, D. A., Zimmerman, F. J., DiGuiseppe, D. L. and McCarty, C. A. (2004). Early television exposure and subsequent attentional problems in children. *Pediatrics*, 113: 708–713.

Cremin, T., Burnard, P. and Craft, A. (2006). Pedagogies of possibility thinking. *International Journal of Thinking Skills and Creativity*, 1(2): 108–119.

Csikszentmihalyi, M. (1996). *Creativity: The Psychology of Discovery and Invention*. London: Harper Collins.

Daintith, J. (ed.) (2009). *A Dictionary of Physics*, 6th edn. Oxford: Oxford University Press.

Dewey, J. (1938). *Experience and Education*. Toronto: Collier-MacMillan Canada Ltd.

DfE. (2014). *Early Years Stage Statutory Framework, Outcomes and Development Matters*. Hampshire: Shurville Publishing.

Hertfordshire ICT Scheme (2012–13). Primary Phase Version 2. Herts County Council, Children's Services ICT Team.

Lauricellaa, A. R., Wartellaa, E., and Rideout, V. J. (2015). Young children's screen time: The complex role of parent and child factors. *Journal of Applied Developmental Psychology*, 36: 11–17.

Meadows, S. (2004). Models of cognition in childhood: Metaphors, achievements and problems. In *The Routeledge Falmer Reader in Psychology of Education*. London: Routledge.

Medwell, J. (2007). *Successful Teaching Placement: Primary and Early Years*. Exeter: Learning Matters.

Moeller, S. (2011). *The World Unplugged*. International Center for Media and the Public Agenda (ICMPA), University of Maryland. https://theworldunplugged.wordpress.com/addictions/conclusions (accessed November 2014).

Morgan, A. (2010). Interactive whiteboards, interactivity and play in the classroom with children aged three to seven years. *European Early Childhood Education Research Journal*, 18(1): 93–104.

Organisation of Economic Cooperation and Development (2001). *Understanding the Digital Divide*. www.oecd.org/sti/1888451.pdf (accessed June 2014).

Palmer, S. (2007). *Toxic Childhood*. London: Orion.

Parten, M. (1932). Social participation among preschool children. *Journal of Abnormal and Social Psychology,* 28(3): 136–147.

Piaget, J. (1952). *The Origins of Intelligence in Children,* 2nd edn. (M. Cook, trans.). (Original work published 1936.) New York: International Universities Press.

Rideout, V. J., Vandewater, E. A. and Wartella, E. A. (2003). *Zero to Six: Electronic Media in the Lives of Infants, Toddlers and Preschoolers.* Kaiser Family Foundation Report. http://files.eric. ed.gov/fulltext/ED482302.pdf (accessed January 2015).

Sawyer, K. (2008). *Group Genius: The Creative Power of Collaboration.* New York: Basic Books.

Sternberg, R. J. (2003). Creative thinking in the classroom. *Scandinavian Journal of Educational Research,* 47(3): 326.

Takacs, Z. K., Swart, E. K. and Bus, A. G. (2015). Benefits and pitfalls of interactive features in technology-enhanced storybooks: A meta-analysis. *Review of Educational Research,* 85(4): 698–739.

Vygotsky, L. (1978). *Mind in Society.* Cambridge, MA: Harvard University Press.

Webb, M. and Cox, M. (2004). A review of the research literature relating to ICT and attainment. *Teaching, Pedagogy and Education,* 13(3): 235–286.

Wood, D. J., Bruner, J. S. and Ross, G. (1976). The role of tutoring in problem solving. *Journal of Child Psychiatry and Psychology,* 17(2): 89–100.

Personal and socio-emotional development and technology

Angela Scollan and Beth Gallagher

Introduction

Children have been, and will continue to be, journeying towards discovering new and unique virtual countries where some adults remain fearful to tread. This is particularly true nowadays when digital technologies make it easier to create and inhabit complex virtual worlds. Simply, it is not possible to return to a time or place without digital technology. The strange dichotomy that exists between parents and their children has been the object of important studies with regards to the use of digital technology. Prensky (2001) coined the term 'digital natives' and 'digital immigrants' to distinguish between the new generation who are immersed and comfortable with digital technology and many adults who have yet to venture forth. Though there has been criticism (Helsper and Eynon, 2010; Steven and Plowman, 2014; Selwyn, 2011) of its binary position, and Prensky now claims it is less relevant, the terms have nonetheless maintained a recognised platform for valuable discourse and further research. Moreover Livingstone (2009) considered the optimistic forces driving digital technology with the endless opportunities for learning, fun, education and development. These, and other studies, reinforce the conclusion that children seem to explore and move between the digital and real world effortlessly while some adults are challenged when making a shift between these contrasting realms and boundaries (Buckingham, 2002; Edwards, 2013a; Marsh, 2010).

Currently, as access to technology for the under-fives have far outreached any research undertaken to fully comprehend long-term socio-emotional and cognitive effects we find ourselves in a dilemma as to trust digital technology or fear it. There is no doubt, as Rubin (2014b) suggests, that technology is here to stay and we are in a new era where digital technology will change how we live, work and play. However, a digital technology paradigm shift has altered our traditional landscapes and crept into daily lives in waves. This chapter will focus on discussing the impact on the personal and socio-emotional development of children of two significant tensions that occur as a result of the transition process between the digital and non-digital worlds, being:

- how practitioners, parents and children protect the personal, socio-emotional well-being of children;
- how practitioners, parents and children manage micro transitions.

Protecting the child

In the context of the importance of new and evolving technologies to the personal and socio-emotional development of children, this chapter will address the merits, myths, fears and facts surrounding its use and impact with a particular focus on 'safeguarding' the child. The Bronfenbrenner Ecological Framework (1979) will be used as a model to inform how systems at macro and micro levels influence and play a role to protect young children from harm.

The merits of technology vis-à-vis social and emotional development

Research, even as early as the 1980s and 1990s, has evidenced increased use of technology and levels of communication through the use of computers (Haughland and Wright, 1997). Moreover, Muller and Perimutter (1985) found that children talked nine times as much while on the computer compared to when working with jigsaws. Plowman *et al.* (2008, 2009) found young children were using a range of technologies within the home and that access across varying socio-economic groups depended more on parental attitudes, family practices and children's own preferences rather than simply on parental income, experiences or competencies. Children playing and learning together on the computer can foster cooperation and a range of social skills including the development of self-concept, sharing, and turn-taking. These findings illustrate a collaborative sociocultural perspective expounded by Vygotsky (1978), whereby learning is enhanced through co-constructing teaching and learning, concluding that a healthy social and emotional development (where needs have been met) will impact positively on learning and achievement. This research shows that technology offers both an opportunity for increased socialisation and quick available access to information and friends; however, a drawback can be that someone can also be socially or virtually present but physically absent. Communication therefore can, to some extent, be limited compared to the physically and socially present friendships in traditional play activities (Beale, 2010 cited in Brown *et al.*, 2013). However, Hamley's toy shop reported that its top-selling toy was a 'wifi connected' doll which evidences children's growing preference for digital play (Smithers, 2014). Yet, Levin and Rosenquest (2001) ask us to consider the possible detrimental impact of the increasing use and role of electronic toys for very young children in the way that quality interactions have been replaced with 'bright lights and bells'.

Therefore Levin and Rosenquest (2001) and Levin (2013) advocate that adults make informed choices with regard to the provision of resources and establish predictable rules and routines for children, to enable them to learn to cooperate and take responsibility for themselves and others in both digital and non-digital realms (see Figure 9.1). This research evidences the growth of technology, but also the limited damaging influence of technology on the social and emotional development of young children with the provision of a safe and nurturing environment.

FIGURE 9.1 Sharing a familiar digital story.

Use of digital technology to ease transitions

It has been well established that secure early attachment is of prime importance to the emotional well-being of children. According to Svanberg (2007), Bowlby described attachment as the 'bond that ties' and as the essential essence of human survival and 'central to our well-being'. It is widely recognised that a confident and resilient disposition relies on an established and healthy early attachment to manage secure transitions.

Practitioners are trained and knowledgeable in managing transitional routines to sensitively and appropriately support young children and their families in a new setting. Research has highlighted how children can be better supported with a transitional object (Winnicott, 1958, 1971, cited in West and Carlson, 2007) and digital technology can be useful as many young children arrive from home with a broad range of technological experiences ranging from the mobile phone, TV controls, and various play resources as discussed above.

Furthermore, since transitioning into a new environment can evoke the most primitive of anxieties and fears, the familiarity of a computer can serve as a comforting and therapeutic tool in the settling-in period. It is therefore crucial to allay the fear in this moment, but also for longer-term emotional development. The transition can be managed so that fears can be 'contained' (Bion, 1962) through the calm reassurance of sensitive practitioners in the presence of significant others, and with familiar and engaging software. This process enables the transition and risk to be more easily tolerated by the child and the parent. A carefully managed transition where anxieties are sufficiently contained in this crucial early stage may elicit a more positive 'memory in feeling' (Klein, 1988) and therefore enable the child to take risks more willingly in the future.

The opportunity arose to observe a three-year-old boy who did not speak English. On his first day he was invited to join the practitioner at the computer. However, she quickly realised that she needed technological support. While she was away, he switched the computer on, chose a program, and was thoroughly absorbed when she returned. She explained to me that he was able to benefit by observing and learning skills in the home from his teenage brother. The familiarity with the computer offered a safe and reassuring 'transitional space' (Scollan and Gallagher, 2013, 2015) for him to acclimatise to the new environment (see Figure 9.2).

FIGURE 9.2 A digital transitional object on his first day at nursery.

It is widely recognised that children have access to a wide range of technologies and that we need to move beyond the question of technology being good or bad for children's development (Marsh and Bishop, 2014; Plowman *et al.*, 2010, 2011; Stephen, 2015) and to lay to rest the polarising of technology versus traditional play. Children need to develop the required competence and confidence to prepare them for safe independent use. Digital technology can equally support and enhance social confidence and emotional resilience as it is embedded in our everyday lives and though it offers educational and fun opportunities it is aligned with elements of risk and harm.

Adult fears and reluctance to use technology

Adults may continue to perceive fear and suspicion and thus lament the 'good old days' of traditional play pursuits for children. Furthermore, many adults have feared that technology would have a negative influence on early emotional and social development and that it would be a threat to physical development such as impact on obesity, lethargy or addictive expressions. Current research at Cambridge University shows how excessive or possibly addictive screen time has detrimental impact on educational attainment (Corder *et al.*, 2015). Additionally, some parents may be anxious that exposure to new information might guide children to accepting different values that might diminish established family morals and cohesion. This latter point was confirmed in meetings with families in a Westminster primary school where one family did not allow exposure to external media other than 'Arabic TV stations', a practice that was shared by others in the group, with one parent making the statement, 'I allow my daughter a laptop now that she is at university'.

Some adults hold on to a historic perception that the internet harbours many invisible dangers and strangers, with Furedi (2008) writing about these fears in his well-known book, *Paranoid Parenting*. Furedi warns of the moral panic, often triggered by the media, impacting a culture of fear among parents for the well-being of their children. Lewis (2014), in her research, reported parents' fears which included increased aggression, obesity, access to inappropriate material, strangers, sexual predators, exposure to conflicting beliefs and values (also supported in the meetings as above). This perception is confirmed by Byron (2010) who states, however, that children live in a risk-averse environment with policies to protect children from the 'slightest possibility of harm'. Therefore, recognising that digital technology is here to stay, adults will have to find ways to overcome the fear of this changing technological landscape so that it can play a positive role in children's development. As such, adults must admit their vital role and responsibility to protect and safeguard young users from an over-use or dependence on the array of games, information and social interactions available through digital technology.

Adapted – Bronfenbrenner's *The Ecology of Human Development* (1979)

The role of adults in protecting children is clear. However, research indicates that more guidance on monitoring and facilitating online environments is needed for policy makers and industry influencers and particularly for adults living and working with children (see Figure 9.3).

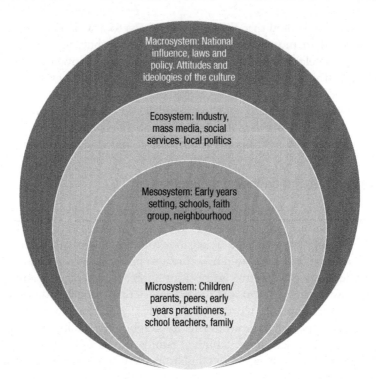

FIGURE 9.3 Protecting children – the role of adults (adapted from Bronfenbrenner's *The Ecology of Human Development*, 1979).

Luke (1999) discussed how the concept of childhood has undergone a rapid transition in the way digital technology is entrenched in childhood experiences. She refers to children as 'techno-literate toddler netizens' of the new millennium. She recognises the pressures on adults to keep abreast of the safeguarding issues and to ensure all children have fair and equal opportunities of access and engagement.

Meyers *et al.* (2010: 7) prompts adults to learn and 'think critically' about the societal expectations of online environments, and argues that the government cannot regulate all internet use. It is further explained that children need explicit supervision and monitoring by adults, as in other play environments throughout childhood.

It therefore follows that a child's safety relies on adults having a clear knowledge and understanding of risk management of digital technology, which will then enable learning, development of resilience and safe independent use to occur. Achieving this aspiration requires adults to hold the positive aspects of digital technology in the balance with any concerns for safety, surveillance, commercialism and possible exploitation.

Managing the use of technology

There is a possibility that managing these risks through increased surveillance would be viewed as a possible infringement of privacy. Lyon (2001) addresses the opposing features of surveillance, care and control. He further expounds the idea that when adults monitor safety, they reduce privacy in an attempt to also manage behaviour. It could be viewed that the monitoring and surveillance of digital technology for children values control over care.

There is a range of literature and guidance for teachers to address the educational needs and risk factors for school-age children and young people. Unfortunately, there is a paucity of information for the under-fives, as it may be assumed that the under-fives can more easily be monitored in their use of digital technology. Additionally, there is a range of filtering systems and software programs to monitor internet use which serve to block selected options such as sexually explicit or violent material. Some software programs offer a watershed period to prevent access to chat rooms or stop users revealing personal details. A well-established reporting website, www.virtualglobaltaskforce.com, acts promptly to support and guide any reports of suspicious or actual online abuse. In all statutory early years settings the internet is securely monitored by filters; however, newly established or smaller private institutions, childminders, home-based carers and parents need to be vigilant to the dangers, as even the best intentioned adults cannot over-see use all the time.

Many children's online sites have self-monitoring expectations such as links to report inappropriate language and behaviours. Marsh (2010) and Meyers *et al.* (2010) in their studies found that key online programs such as Club Penguin, Barbie Girls and Pixie Hollow are designed with safety, privacy and security as a priority. For example, Club Penguin (www.clubpenguin.com) monitors users' conversations and picks up any abusive language and conversations, but like many internet sites it relies on self and peer monitoring too. Adults have a role to guide children in using these safeguarding features and develop accountability for themselves and others.

Younger siblings can also be exposed to inappropriate material, language and narratives used by older siblings and parents (refer to the case study above involving the three-year-old child). It will be more challenging, in these situations, to measure the impact on children's emotional and social development.

It is clear that one of the most important roles of parents and practitioners in these modern times is to safeguard children, and despite the lack of central guidance there are increasingly more and more tools available so that children can continue to reap the rewards that digital technology offers. It must be admitted that digital technology today is widespread and pervasive in our society. Although there should be a rightful concern about safeguarding and protection from the negative aspects of digital technology, it should also be recognised that over-protection can inhibit opportunities for children to learn to manage risk, and in addition impact their privacy and voice (Donavan and Katz 2009 cited in Meyers *et al.*, 2010). Furthermore, these views can hinder children from realising the full benefits of digital technology.

Protecting children – the role of industry

Industry has a critical role to fulfil to support adults in their quest to protect children; however, these issues pose a particular concern for industry as it manages the tensions between the demands of children (key stakeholders), parents as gatekeepers, and its own profitability. It can therefore be challenging to achieve all goals, as a focus on one feature may constrain the other.

Undoubtedly, industry will need to address the competing value systems as different stakeholders may have different views and priorities. Lyon (2001) explains how, for example, a value and need of one stakeholder (for example, the parent's assurance of a safe environment) may conflict with the needs and rights of the direct stakeholder (for example, the child). Furthermore, the stakes may rise as the child grows. Additionally, parents want safe sites for the purpose of constraining another stakeholder (for example, the paedophile who wants the freedom to groom children), again conflicting with the key stakeholder (for example, the child). Quite simply, in the case of children, they value fun and social communication with peers, but adults place equal value on safety. As in any other environment, children need to learn to respect others, and be vigilant to dangers to self and others.

Furthermore, Lyon (2001) draws our attention to the commercial ventures of the gaming world which relies on sales and places pressure on consumers to invest in memberships and publicly tally the levels of investment with display panels. This results in easily identifiable levels of privilege and disparity. In turn, parents cannot be protected from the subsequent pressures from children using 'pester power', which results from powerful marketing tactics.

Although industry has a vested interest in safety, it generally advocates that user training and adult supervision is necessary to ensure the safety of children. Livingstone (2009) claims that the safety of children has become a common societal expectation. Byron (2010) recognises that children can become their own gatekeepers. She further concludes that in order to ensure that children are equipped with knowledge of safety concerns they should be provided with 'teachable moments' and instruction in what it means to be a 'good cyber-citizen'. Byron also suggests that there should be a balance established between parental anxiety and children's privacy, and also calls on adults to be responsible, as 'we are all citizens of the web'.

Protecting children – the role of national and European influencers

Although adults and industry have important roles to play in safeguarding children, national organisations exist which also support this effort. The Child Exploitation and Online Protection Centre (CEOP) offers video links guiding practice for practitioners and parents to help protect children from online abuse. One such video is an eight-minute animation aimed at children from reception/Key Stage 1 (four to six years) to show children how to protect themselves, respect other users and when to tell a known adult of any moments when they feel fearful with 'butterflies in the tummy'.

In 2007, the UK government commissioned the Byron Report, which served to recognise that the internet is used by children across the age range so as to benefit learning and development but also therein lays accessible material which is inappropriate for children. The Report avoided entering into discussion surrounding the potential consequential social and emotional harm from digital technology, but addressed how the media could be used to enhance positive learning experiences. The Report was well received by parents, practitioners and government representatives but had a mixed reception from the video industry and this prompted an action plan (June, 2008). The follow-up review, 'Do we have safer children in a digital world?', published in March 2010 indicated that great strides in the UK had taken place to inform parents and practitioners about how they could both protect children but also empower them to self-monitor their safety. This review was followed up with the establishment of the UK Council for Child Internet Safety (UKCCIS) whereby more than 200 organisations have agreed to work in partnership to promote safe use of digital technologies. Guidance has been produced that promotes effective safety measures for industry, clear parental control filters for home broadband users, and a 'friendly WiFi logo' (www.gov.uk). Additionally, 'Positive Online Content and Services for Children in Europe' (POSCON) offer guidelines for producers and designers, in line with Article 13 of the UN Convention on the Rights of the Child, to ensure children are enabled to access quality materials and safe learning experiences.

Transitions between digital and non-digital worlds

While there is research acknowledging the impact technology has on the socio-emotional child (Siraj-Blatchford and Siraj-Blatchford, 2006; Morgan and Siraj-Blatchford, 2013; Levin, 2013; Marsh, 2010), little research has been undertaken regarding the emotional impact of transitioning between digital and non-digital realms and even less during the micro transitions children experience. Moving between realms has an impact on emotional development, behaviour, self-regulation, resilience, empathy and social skills, although it is still uncharted territory when we consider 'how' children are impacted (Buckingham, 2002; Goleman, 1996; Marsh, 2010; Rubin, 2014a; Siraj-Blatchford and Siraj-Blatchford, 2006).

Micro transition identification (what does it look like in practice?)

Ashforth *et al.* (2000) use the term 'micro role transition' to capture psychological movements between engagement and disengagement of one's role. We use the concept of micro transition in this chapter to mean the movement of the child between digital and non-digital worlds physically, cognitively and/or emotionally (Scollan and Gallagher, 2013). Micro transitions are small changes or shifts, either physically or cognitively, when a child reinvents experiences or changes their agenda. The term micro transition is more than a role or engagement; it is underpinned by self, choice and exploration. The role of the adult to recognise and support a child during micro transitions will vary greatly depending upon training, experience and perspective. For instance, if an adult working with children has a fear of technology or has reached their digital ceiling then let us consider if it will make a difference if digital fear is only recognised; recognised and understood; or recognised, understood and actively acknowledged so that consciousness of our personal cut-off points do not prevent us, in our professional roles, from offering high-quality learning opportunities (see Chapter 5).

Bronfenbrenner (1979) identifies transition as occurring when an individual's position is altered as the result of a change in role, environment or circumstance. Bronfenbrenner's Ecological Systems Theory captures the transition occurring in a child's world at local, national and global levels as part of their everyday life experience, while accessing early years provision and resources. Brooker (2008) and Petriwskyj *et al.* (2005) develop Bronfenbrenner's Ecological Systems Theory further by arguing that transition is an ever-evolving process of 'mutual adaptations' moving between environments and developmental stages from both the familiar to the unfamiliar. Brooker (2008) recognises that multidimensional characteristics and traits within any transition process or experience require high-quality support and management by both the child and practitioner. Dimensional characteristics during digital and non-digital transitions are identified as emotive and social reactions, with communication and knowledge being transferred between worlds to accommodate and assimilate new understanding to extend knowledge (Levin, 2013; Levin-Gelman, 2014; Marsh, 2010; Marsh and Bishop, 2014; Brooker, 2008). Therefore, a pedagogical model to consider 'how' adults can recognise and support micro transitions during everyday activities, when non-virtual reality becomes virtual reality for the child, will be discussed here.

Oatley (1990) argues that it is only in the twentieth century that the need for adults to know the difference between 'self' and their professional or societal 'role' became evident. Dewey (1966), Oatley (1990) and Schön (1987) advocate the necessity for individuals to be able to differentiate and consciously reflect on self, role and impact regarding the ability to cope with change. If those interacting with children perceive their role to be fixed or emerging, then their perspective will impact greatly on how digital exploration is supported and understood, thus impacting upon a child's learning, emotional development and well-being.

Digital development

Rubin (2014b) identifies digital technology as a way of life that develops skills and tools vital to decode, survive and problem-solve previously unknown realms, dimensions and worlds. Edwards (2013b) and Levin (2013) prompt debate regarding media influence to question whether digital technology is positive for children's development, to provoke adults to consider 'how and what' it is that children and adults learn from each other and independently during their interaction with digital technology. *Who is teaching who* is an area to reflect upon when it comes to digital development and progression. For instance, those more knowledgeable or naturally capable in the use of digital equipment are amazing to observe both physically and cognitively while engaging with technical challenges to coordinate digital worlds and tools. Children may observe adult technical skills, although perhaps it is adults who need to learn how to explore and observe children while interacting with these emerging new realms, waves and micro transitions (Brown *et al.*, 2013; Edwards, 2013b; Marsh, 2010; Prensky, 2001; Rubin 2014a).

Digital engagement

Research undertaken by BECTA (2008, 2010), Marsh (2010), Plowman and Stephen (2005), Levin (2013) and Levin (2014) recognises the need for trained practitioners to be aware of the multidimensional skills and learning opportunities accessible to children via digital engagement. Practitioners can use observation and sustained shared communication to assess how a child's socio-emotional, physical, technical and cognitive skills are developing and extended during digital engagement. There is a need for adults to support physical use of technology while understanding how cognitive engagement stimulates children's young minds. For instance, Levin (2013) and Levin-Gelman (2014) identify that adults cannot ignore their role and responsibility to understand and probe into cognitive development and brain capacity while entering the virtual world without considering the impact it will have upon the child's emotional development. While digital tools can also be used to occupy or appease children's interest or attention so that adults can 1) find space to relax, 2) follow their own agenda, 3) follow direction of a curricula, it is evident that without knowledge or insight into the realms of personal and socio-emotional exploration and transition, opportunities are missed by adults to decode the inner world of dual learning between the digital and non-digital world for children. Consequently, while adults may have their own agenda for the use of digital resources it is apparent that the child's agenda might not be the same.

Digital agenda, emotional aftermath and transition space

When a child has been engaged at highly attuned, emotive and concentrated levels while immersed in technology, there is opportunity for adults to consider not only learning but the emotional 'aftermath' (Scollan and Gallagher, 2013). Emotional aftermath is the build-up of physical, creative and cognitive energy children amass within digital realms and transfer back into the non-digital world. This identified *aftermath* provokes us to question if an emotional space exists between interaction with technology and the thinking about it during and afterwards. Subsequently, adults are encouraged to reflect on and be mindful of the transitional space required for both cognitive and emotional equilibrium between activities and changes in thinking and feelings (Dunn, 1988; Dunn and Ploumin, 1990; Goleman, 1996). To this end we propose adults manage and reflect upon impending highs, potential isolation or danger inherent within the virtual world. Or do we?

Educational use of digital resources upon socio-emotional development

Recent research literature at Boston University by Radesky *et al.* (2015) questions the intended educational use of digital resources, provoking adults to consider if technology is used by adults to divert children's attention or as a tool to manage them, their emotions and their behaviour, in order to reinforce an adult agenda. Radesky *et al.* provoke further debate by recognising that the impact of young children accessing screen time via current multiple modalities offers infinite interactive possibilities that are in stark contrast to children accessing interactive television. They recognise the need for research to substantiate the impact screen time has and will have upon young children and lives. There is a concern that less adult and child interaction during solo use of technology is detrimental to long-term social and emotional development. If interaction and communication is impacted upon, who should we be concerned for – the child, adult or future society? It is indeed possible that Prensky's (2001) digital immigrant may fear being left behind by the digital native because children are embracing digital technology much faster than adults.

It is pertinent to question at this point if generational gazumping between childhood experiences offers insight and pathways into digital realms at a faster pace depending on the technology interacted with during our childhoods. For instance, Sutton-Smith (2001) defined the concept of play many times by referring to his own childhood memories and experiences of play to challenge the many dimensions and meaning of play. Subsequently, it is not that adults or children are more advanced, but it is perhaps that adults do not have the hindsight or memories of digital technology embedded within their childhood play or memories. If adults have not been immersed in digital play and realms it is challenging to assess exactly where, what and how children are learning during digital exploration.

A pedagogical model that underpins this chapter is the PEEP model, which can be used to reflect on and demonstrate how provision develops digital skills that impact upon a child's personal, social and emotional (PSE) development. The PEEP model is a tool to reflect upon practice and interactions to explore micro transition and 'emotional space' between the physical environment and inner worlds entered by children and practitioners during the use of digital resources. PEEP pedagogy is broken down into four areas consisting of 1) provision, 2) environment, 3) engagement, 4) protection, to formulate a pedagogical lens that identifies challenges presented during digital interactions (see Table 9.1).

The PEEP model aims to provoke reflection regarding communication, actions and reactions, emotional literacy and physical movement experienced by children during micro transitions and digital use. Reflection on practice, digital expectations and values are presented in the model to evaluate observable interactions to learn alongside those acclimatised into Rubin's (2014b) new technology wave and era.

TABLE 9.1 PEEP model (Scollan and Gallagher, 2015): reflective prompts for practitioner, parents and children to discuss

Provision	Environment	Engagement	Protection
Reflect and discuss:	**Reflect and discuss:**	**Reflect and discuss:**	**Reflect and discuss:**
How are digital learning opportunities planned and assessed to support social and emotional skills?	Define a stimulating and creative digital environment.	What do we mean by digital engagement?	Where have identified rules or routines derived from in your environment? For instance, are digital rules inherited from another class, environment, person or ideal? Why can two or four children use DT at a given time? Who is this rule for? What is the rule protecting against?

Provision	Environment	Engagement	Protection
Reflect and discuss:	**Reflect and discuss:**	**Reflect and discuss:**	**Reflect and discuss:**
When digital equipment is purchased who chooses it and what is the rationale of making it available to children?	How does the digital environment differ from the non-digital environment?	Should digital engagement be verbal or non-verbal? Why?	Whilst 'protecting' children in the digital environment, identify exactly what children are in danger from?
How does digital technology offered to children support learning? For instance, what purpose does it have?	How are emotional and social spaces supported? For instance, is there a planned space, time or pedagogical strategy for children to accommodate and manage micro transitions between digital and non-digital play?	Should engagement in and between the digital realms be adult or child led? Why? What is the purpose of adult engagement when children use DT? For instance, reflect on previous interactions you have had with children to consider what the 'real' agenda was.	Reflect on the last time you used the term 'protection from harm' or 'danger' linked to DT. What risk did you identify and what were the main risks and your concerns? Why did you have these concerns?
Who takes responsibility for digital resources in your environment?			
Who should be accountable for digital resources and provision? Why?	How are micro transitions identified and supported?	Was the engagement driven by outcomes, routines, assessment, natural curiosity or sustained and meaningful discussion?	Reflect upon, discuss and compare a real concern in comparison to 'inherited' concerns?
How is provision you offer digitally enabling?	How are digital home environments represented in the setting? Should they be? Why?		Reflect if the level of protection in your environment is digitally enabling or disabling? How? Why?
Should all practitioners know the purpose and potential of digital technology upon a child's learning and PSE development?	Is the environment digitally enabling? How? Define what a micro transition looks like. For instance, when do you notice children moving between digital and non-digital realms or environments?	How does your practice and relationship with children positively support digital engagement? Are adult relationships and skills in your environment digitally enabling? How?	How can digital immigrants protect digital natives? Identify if both are needed to be involved as partners towards safeguarding
How is this managed within your environment?			
How are staff and resources deployed to support digital development and skills for all children?	Reflect how micro transitions impact upon the environment, learning opportunities and level of engagement in the setting? For instance, how does digital technology relate to other areas of learning?	Reflect upon and discuss digital observations undertaken to assess what has been measured as significant and why? Is there a range and breadth of: technical or physical skill; creativity; cognitive processes; PSE milestones; contextualised knowledge and understanding?	Identify exact safeguarding skills children are supported to develop in your environment. For instance, how do adults discuss or explain safeguarding strategies and awareness with children?

Digital technology and the socio-emotional child

The socio-emotional child entering digital worlds – how does this manifest back into the real world?

We begin to apply the PEEP model by exploring early years provision impacting upon social interactions and emotional development within the digital realms. Relationships with others, and the social skills we need to fit into our media and digital-thirsty culture can, as Prensky (2001), Marsh (2010) and Levin (2013) argue, present indirect generational conflict. For instance, young children who are born into our media-rich world are born with the 'apps' to interact with it, seemingly, so naturally. Prensky (2001) argues that adults who have immigrated into the digital arena find transition at times a challenge. Adults can become so exhausted and fatigued when trying to keep up with new technology that they reach a 'cut-off' point of trying to understand new waves of technology. Rubin (2014b) acknowledges the arrival of an intense 'digital realm' that is upon us 'that is so immersive that it is neurologically indistinguishable from the outside world' (Rubin, 2014b). The PEEP model aims to provoke reflection on adult impact by questioning the purpose of digital resources.

There are many implicit and explicit boundaries, expectations and interactions between the digital and non-digital worlds which, at times, are complex to observe and decode. BECTA (2008) and Edwards (2013a) capture the intriguing concept of 'how' adults in the non-digital world can enter a child's inner digital world at the right time, to offer support, guidance or social perspective. BECTA (2008), Edwards (2013b) and Stephen and Plowman (2008) recognise the need for attuned, skilful professionals who are able to manage digital exploration and multidimensional learning opportunities effectively (see Chapter 6). The PEEP model aims to provoke reflection for adults to explore digital pedagogy and impact because knowing when or how to enter a child's virtual exploration is a challenge.

For instance, the cartoon *Rugrats* offers us insight into a child's creative and imaginative worlds with examples of adult perspective from characters who are not immersed in the child's world, but are merely observers, sometimes worlds apart. The adult observers 'Uncle Stu' and 'Grandpa' perceive the group of children playing as safe, happy, engaged and busy, although the children's experiences at that same instant are in vast contrast to the adult observers' perceptions. Chuckie is hanging on for dear life with one finger, hanging from the highest cliff edge in the Himalayas and there is a scary Yeti monster, who is best friends with Angelica, just about to eat him or, at the very least, bite off his head! Phil and Lil are Chuckie's twin friends and are concocting a possible life-saving strategy to save Chuckie with only seconds left. The twins discuss various strategies using previous trial-and-error experiences to devise a plan. They hold a moral and ethical discussion regarding Angelica, who is sometimes their friend and sometimes their enemy. Currently she has sided with the Yeti, adding to the whole dilemma…

How, indeed, can inner worlds entered during digital or creative moments be fully understood or supported by adult observers? A child's communication and translation of events during highly emotive or challenging dilemmas will manifest within the non-digital world. Children will continue their adventures outside of digital constraints to transfer their emotions and feelings into their present environment to test out ideas, previous experiences or unfinished exploration. This continuation from one world to the other is identified as a micro transition and will require 'emotional space' (ES) to manifest. How this space is acknowledged, provided for and who it is supported by, are aspects within everyday experiences about which the PEEP model aims to provoke reflection and discussion.

Behaviour changes during digital transition or agenda

As discussed earlier in the chapter, emotional tension and aftermath between digital transition can develop for many reasons for both children and adults. For instance, adults who intend to use digital equipment for a technical purpose to develop children's use of the camera or extend literacy skills using a prescribed educational package may become frustrated when children exceed the task or technical mastery with ease to go well beyond the adult's planned intention or next step.

Children may utilise well-planned activities and digital technology offered by adults as a pivot for something else and a clash of digital agenda may occur. The PEEP model prompts reflection concerning digital clash or agenda that will need to be managed by the child or adult depending on reactions within the environment provoked from emotions or by behaviour. Notwithstanding, as BECTA and Rubin (2014a, b) argue, it is vital for reflective practitioners to acknowledge tension, challenges and possible digital 'clashes' of agenda to recognise:

■ how they are dealt with and managed;

■ the long-term impact on the learning environment, child's behaviour, motivation level and learning opportunities;

■ pedagogy shift so that practitioners learn alongside, with and from the child;

■ the development of digital resilience.

The PEEP model and reflective practice

Aim to apply the PEEP model to reflect on recent interactions observed relating to digital activities. Consider if an activity was a positive experience or not. And, if identified as a positive experience, who was it positive for? How do you know the resource or activity was positive or beneficial for the child? Who took the lead? Who taught who? Who initiated the use of digital resources? It's pertinent to contemplate while applying the PEEP model if adults and children share similar digital agendas, goals or digital language. For instance, how can the adult listen, communicate and observe the child who has entered, left or is transitioning between digital and non–digital realms? Finally, while we reflect upon micro transitions, space and digital realms we need to consider what has *not* been identified or *seen* through the eyes of the observer. What has not been measured? Is there an 'unseen emotional environment and space' between the inner digital world and external environment? How can we be sure it is there?

Case study

The following case study presents examples of how social and emotional skills naturally develop during child-initiated digital exploration. Emotional space offers children the opportunity to master new skills between digital and non-digital worlds. The space offers time to position oneself and make sense of rules and boundaries required to decode, make sense, explore, creatively own, assimilate and master outcomes within digital realms that observers may be unaware of. The PEEP model can be applied to the following scenario to consider:

- micro transitions;
- unseen emotional environments and space;
- child and adult roles.

During a recent visit to a nursery two children aged three and four years were observed sitting at a PC choosing to embark on a 'vampire' package and every time they found three words starting with the letter 'v', the vampire gave a deep and scary long laugh. The two children squealed with delight, thoroughly enjoying being scared while observing each other's reaction and facial contortions. Enthusiastic screams were undertaken simultaneously with both children theatrically trying to be the most scared, scariest and alarmed. In fact, a competition to outdo each other could even be seen erupting to combine their unique reactions and experiences. The sheer joy they displayed during this activity enticed another four children to join them. Child A continued to control the mouse, child B continued to point to the words on the screen beginning with the letter 'v', while children C, D, E and F, who had recently joined the activity, interacted, colluded, negotiated, problem-solved and swapped vampire scary stories from a recent TV programme and birthday party they had experienced.

Interestingly, in the above scenario children were observed immersed in the vampire game moving between the virtual world and within a split second without any notice would enter back into the non-digital world and physical environment (a micro transition). The group of children seemed to effortlessly understand their shared, natural 'micro transitions'. As an observer it takes time to decode and understand micro transition and the emotional space that children enter. Reflexivity (Bolton, 2010) offers opportunities to consciously be aware of the 'self' during observation of others because our agenda to observe will impact upon what we see (Dewey, 1966). Bruce (2012) recognises how observers learn about the rules and rituals children follow, only if the observer is ready to learn or be led by the child. Notwithstanding, micro transitions can only be explored by observers who are tuned into a child's agenda. Observers who enter a child's world have much to decode with regards to meaning, places and spaces. Children enter virtual worlds naturally in micro seconds and the transition can be so fast it is unseen. For instance, adults who focus on their own agenda, curricula or goal-driven outcomes form their own reality or 'space' which differs from that of the child. Reality in the environment can be adult centred, which is in contrast to that of the child's. Reality realms can envelope adults into habitual zones of practice to prevent seeing the real child and worlds they enter.

Child D is observed to be immersed and excited during the above 'vampire' scenario and seems to be enjoying the interaction with peers and the vampire play. An adult in the nursery joins the group to reiterate the nursery rules that only two children at a time should be using the computer. Four children (including child D) are encouraged to leave the computer area and join in with a planned activity close by. The group disbanded and instantly the richness of the world they had entered shifted. Child D continued to laugh while using a substantial vampire voice, physically making vampire movements to continue his exploration. His play and agenda seemed to continue with or without the computer and his creative and cognitive skills applied during the observed 'vampire play' were transferred between the digital realm and into the physical, non-digital world. The transition was fast. The adult asked child D to stop using a loud voice while he created flying actions, swishing around and flapping on a curtain.

Reflecting on the above scenario, child D displayed sustained concentration periods during vampire play, engaged with peers and creatively interacted with the content of the computer package while managing rules of both the digital and non-digital worlds. For instance, he managed game rules while contributing towards construction of new ones and added to the vampire play and new direction the game was moving towards. He alternated between the digital and non-digital realms effortlessly and while immersed in digital play, he left when asked and moved to the area suggested by the adult. In the non-digital realm child D continued the vampire theme, transferring the play into a more physical form. Micro transitions produce various levels of emotional aftermath requiring adults to offer space or time so that children have opportunity to assimilate their thinking, behaviour and 'physicalness' between both realms. Do children receive space and recognition for skills developed? Refer to the PEEP model to consider what this adult 'did not see' and discuss the impact this may have on the child's well-being and behaviour.

The above examples capture how micro transitions between the digital and non digital realms occur continuously during everyday interactions in order to consider how children manage their own learning, curiosity, behaviour and life skills. Adults need to be mindful of unforeseen emotional space between these two worlds, which is a hybrid space where the digital and non-digital worlds collide.

DISCUSSION TOPICS

- How is transition between the virtual and real world defined within practice and given 'space'?
- Identify the role of the practitioner to support emotional development or aftermath during transition between both worlds.
- Reflect upon strategies that can be used to empower and prepare children to safeguard themselves within the digital world.

Conclusion

This chapter concludes that new and evolving technologies are important to the personal, social and emotional development of children, and that we will need to accept that they are here to stay. In this context, proper safeguarding is particularly relevant regarding accountability to protect self and others. The Bronfenbrenner Ecological Framework (1979) is useful as a model to inform national organisations, practitioners and parents of their intended roles and accountability in the protection of children. By doing so, the learning and development of children will be protected and enhanced. Micro transitions will inevitably occur between digital and non-digital exploration and by applying the PEEP model at micro level adults can observe interactions and communication to be aware of these digital realms. These processes can identify, support and manage the emotional and social space and development that impact on children in their learning and play.

This chapter and book has ventured to share a journey along a road less travelled by many adults and to offer support for practitioners and parents in their roles of guiding, interacting and educating children in their digital developments. As adults we might romanticise yesteryears' traditional play experiences but digital play has become the 'real play' of today. We cannot know the world our children will inhabit as adults. As Khalil Gibran (1923/1991) famously wrote about our children of tomorrow, 'your children are not your children, you may house their bodies but not their souls, for their souls dwell in the house of tomorrow which you cannot visit, not even in your dreams'. So today, let us join children and learn alongside them on their digital journey.

References

Ashforth, B., Kreiner, G., and Fugate, M. (2000). *The Academy of Management Review,* 25(3): 472–491.

BECTA (2008). *Harnessing Technology: Next Generation Learning 2008–14*, DCSF (webarchive. nationalarchives.gov.uk).

BECTA (2010). *Digital Literacy: Teaching Critical Thinking for Our Digital World.* www.archive. teachfind.com/becta/schools.becta.org (accessed March 2016).

Bion, W. R. (1962). *Learning form Experience.* London: Heineman. (Reprinted London: Karnac.)

Bolton, G. (2010). *Reflective Practice: Writing and Professional Development.* London: Sage.

Bowlby, J. (1969). *Attachment: Attachment and Loss, Vol. 1.* New York: Basic Books.

Bronfenbrenner, U. (1974). *A Report on Longitudinal Evaluations of Preschool Programs. Vol 2: Is Early Intervention Effective?* Washington, DC: DH.

Bronfenbrenner, U. (1979). *The Ecology of Human Development.* Cambridge MA: Harvard University Press.

Brooker, L. (2005). Learning to be a child: Cultural diversity and early years ideology. In N. Yelland (ed.), *Critical Issues in Early Childhood Education.* Maidenhead: Open University Press.

Brooker, L. (2008). *Supporting Transitions in the Early Years.* London: Open University Press.

Brown, J., Winsor, D. L. and Blake, S. (2013). Technology and social-emotional development in early childhood environments. Cited in S. Blake, D. L. Winsor and L. Allen, *Child Development and the Use of Technology: Perspective, Applications and Experiences.* Hershey, PA: Information Science Reference.

Bruce, T. (2012). *Early Childhood Practice.* London: Sage.

Buckingham, D. (2002). *Small Screens: Television for Children (Studies in Communication and Society).* London: Leicester University Press.

Byron, T. (2008). *Safer Children in a Digital World: The Report of the Byron Review.* webarchive. nationalarchives.gov.uk

Byron, T. (2010). *Do We Have Safer Children in a Digital World? A Review of Progress since the 2008 Byron Review.* webarchive.nationalarchives.gov.uk

Child Exploitation and Online Protection Centre (CEOP): www.ceop.police.uk (accessed March 2016).

Corder, K., Atkin, A. J., Bamber, D. J., Brage, S., Dunn, V. J., Ekelund, U., Owens, M., van Slujis, E. M. F. and Goodyer, I. M. (2015). Revising on the run or studying on the sofa: Prospective associations between physical activity, sedentary behaviour, and exam results in British adolescents. *International Journal of Behavioural Nutrition and Physical Activity*, 12(1): 106.

Dewey, J. (1966). *Selected Educational Writing.* London: Heinemann.

Dowling, M. (2005). *Young Children's Personal, Social and Emotional Development*, 2nd edn. London: Paul Chapman.

Dunn, J. (1988). *The Beginnings of Social Understanding.* Oxford: Basil Blackwell.

Dunn, J. and Ploumin, R. (1990). *Separate Lives: Why Siblings Are So Different.* London: Basic Books.

Edwards, S. (2013a). By-passing the debate beyond the 'technology question' in the early years. http://tactyc.org.uk/pdfs/Reflection-Edwards.pdf

Edwards, S. (2013b). Digital play in the early years: A contextual response to the problem of integrating digital technologies and play-based learning in the early childhood curriculum. *European Early Childhood Education Research Journal*, 21(2), 199–212.

Edwards, S. (2014). Towards contemporary play: Sociocultural theory and the digital-consumerist context. *Journal of Early Childhood Research*, 12(3): 219–233.

Furedi, F. (2008). *Paranoid Parenting.* London: Bloomsbury.

Gibran, K. (1923/1991). *The Prophet.* London: Pan Books.

Goleman, D. (1996). *Emotional Intelligence.* London: Bloomsbury.

Goleman, D. (1999). *Working With Emotional Intelligence.* London: Bloomsbury.

Haughland, S. W. and Wright, J. C. (1997). *Young Children and Technology: A World of Discovery.* Needham Heights, MA: Allyn & Bacon.

Helsper, E. and Eynon, R. (2011). Digital natives: Where is the evidence? *British Educational Research Journal*, 36(3): 503–520.

Klein, M. (1988). *Love, Guilt and Reparation and Other Works, 1921–1945.* London: Virago.

Levin, D. E. (2013). *Beyond Remote-Controlled Childhood: Teaching Children in the Media Age.* Washington, DC: NAEYC.

Levin, D. and Rosenquest, B. (2001). The increasing role of electronic toys in the lives of infants and toddlers: Should we be concerned? *Contemporary Issues in Early Childhood*, 2(2): 242–247.

Levin, D. E. and Kilbourne, J. (2009). *So Sexy So Soon: The New Sexualised Childhood and What Parents Can Do to Protect their Kids.* New York: Ballantine Books.

Levin-Gelman, D. (2014). *Design for Kids: Digital Products for Playing and Learning.* New York: Rosenfeld Media.

Lewis, B. (2014). *Raising Children in a Digital Age.* Oxford: Lion Hudson.

Livingstone, S. (2009). *Children and the Internet: Great Expectation, Challenging Realities.* Cambridge: Polity.

Luke, C. (1999). What next? Toddler netizens, Playstation thumb, techno-literacies. *Contemporary Issues in Early Childhood*, 1(1): 95–100.

Lyon, D. (2001). *Surveillance Society: Monitoring Everyday Life* (Issues in Society Series). Buckingham: Open University Press.

Marsh, J. (2010). Young children's play in online virtual worlds. *Journal of Research*, 8(1): 23–39.

Marsh, J. and Bishop, J. (2014). *Changing Play: Play, Media and Commercial Culture from the 1950s to the Present Day*. Buckingham: Open University Press.

Meyers, E. M., Nathan, L. P. and Unsworth, K. (2010). Who's watching your kids? Safety and surveillance in virtual worlds for children. *Journal of Virtual Worlds Research*, 3(2): 3–28.

Morgan, A. and Siraj-Blatchford, J. (2013). *Using ICT in the Early Years: Parents and Practitioners in Partnership*. London: Practical Pre-School Books.

Muller, A. A. and Perlmutter, M. (1985). Pre-school children's problem-solving interactions at computers and jigsaw puzzles. *Journal of Applied Developmental Psychology*, 6: 173–186.

Nuffield Foundation. www.nuffieldfoundation.org/news/disadvantaged-three-and-four-year-olds-losing-out-good-quality-nursery-provsion (accessed May 2015).

Oatley, K. (1990). Cited in Ashforth, B. E. (2012). *Role Transitions in Organizational Life: An Identity-Based Perspective*. East Sussex: Routledge.

Petriwskyj, A., Thorpe, K. and Tayler, C. (2005). Trends in construction of transition to school in three western regions. *International Journal of Early Years Education*, 13(1): 55–69.

Plowman, L. and Stephen, C. (2005). Children, play and computers in pre-school education. *British Journal of Education Technology*, 36(2): 145–157.

Plowman, L., Stephen, C. and McPake, J. (2008). Just picking it up? Young children learning with technology in the home. *Cambridge Journal of Education*, 38(3): 303–319.

Plowman, L., Stephen, C. and McPake, J. (2009). *Growing Up with Technology: Young Children Learning in a Digital World*. London: Routledge.

Plowman, L., McPake, J. and Stephen, C. (2010). The technologisation of childhood? Young children and technology in the home. *Children and Society*, 24(1): 63–74.

Plowman, L., Stevenson, O., McPake, J., Stephen, C. and Adey, C. (2011). Parents, preschoolers and learning with technology at home: Some implications for policy. *Journal of Computer Assisted Learning*, 27(4): 361–371.

Positive Online Content and Services for Children in Europe: www.positivecontent.eu

Prensky, M. (2001). Digital natives, digital immigrants. *On the Horizon*, 9(5), October 2001.

Radesky, J. S., Schumacher, J. and Zuckerman, B. (2015). Mobile and interactive media use by young children: The good, the bad, and the unknown. *Pediatrics*, 135(1): 1–3.

Rubin, E. (2014a). *Legal Education in the Digital Age*. New York: Cambridge University Press.

Runin, E. (2014b). Cited in J. V. Pavlick (ed.) (2016). *Digital Technology and the Future of Broadcasting: Global Perspectives*. London: Routledge.

Schön, D. A. (1987). *Educating the Reflective Practitioner: Towards a New Design for Teaching and Learning in the Professions*. San Francisco: Jossey-Bass.

Scollan, A. and Gallagher, B. (2013). EDU3307 Lecture 20. Emotional aftermath and digital transition. Lecture presented at Middlesex University, 2013.

Scollan, A. and Gallagher, B. (2015). Paddling in the digital wave. Paper presented at the fourth Symposium 'Children's Cultures, Well-being and Digital Society', School of Education and Continuing Studies, University of Portsmouth, 10 July 2015.

Selwyn, N. (2011). *Education and Technology: Key Issues and Debates*. London: Continuum.

Sharp, P. (2002). *Nurturing Emotional Literacy*. London: David Fulton.

Siraj-Blatchford, I. and Manni, L. (2007). *Effective Leadership in the Early Years Sector: The ELEYS Study, London*. Institute of Education: University of London.

Siraj-Blatchford, I. and Siraj-Blatchford, J. (2006). *A Curriculum Development Guide to ICT in Early Childhood Education*. Nottingham: Trentham Books with Early Education.

Siraj-Blatchford, I. and Wong, Y. (1999). Defining and evaluating 'quality' – early childhood education in an international context: dilemmas and possibilities. *Early Years: An International Journal of Research and Development*, 20(1): 7–18.

Siraj-Blatchford, I., Sylva, K., Muttock, S., Gilden, R. and Bell, D. (2002). *Researching Effective Pedagogy in the Early Years*. DfES research report 536. London: Department for Education and Skills.

Smithers, R. (2014). Small wonder: Hi-tech doll. *The Guardian*, 27 June, p35.

Stephen, C. (2015). Keynote: Taking another look: the affordances of new technologies for early childhood education. 25th EECERA Annual Conference, Innovation, Experimentation and Adventure In Early Childhood, Barcelona, Catalunya, Spain, 7–10 September 2015.

Stephen, C. and Plowman, L. (2008). Enhancing Learning with ICT in Preschool. *Early Child Development and Care*, 178(6): 637–654.

Stephen, C. and Plowman, L. (2014). Digital play. In Brooker, L., Blaise, M. and Edwards, S. (eds), *Play and Learning in Early Childhood*. London: Sage.

Stewart, N. and Pugh, R. (2007). *Early Years Vision in Focus, Part 2: Exploring Pedagogy*. Shrewsbury: Shropshire County Council.

Sutton-Smith, B. (2001). *The Ambiguity of Play*. Cambridge, MA: Harvard University Press.

Svanberg, P. O. (2007). *Attachment in Practice*. Newcastle: Siren Film and Video Ltd.

UK Council for Child Internet Safety (UKCCIS): http://education.gov.uk/ukccis (accessed April 2015).

Vygotsky, L. S. (1978). *Mind in Society*. Cambridge, MA: Harvard University Press.

West, L. and Carlson, A. (2007). *Claiming Space: An In-Depth Auto-Biographical Study of a Local Sure Start Project 2001–2006*. Canterbury: Canterbury Christ Church University.

Index